T0050518

Temple Antiquities

The Templar Papers II

Temple Antiquities

The Templar Papers II

Oddvar Olsen

BOOKS

Winchester, UK
Washington, USA

First published by O-Books, 2010
O-Books is an imprint of John Hunt Publishing Ltd., Laurel House, Station Approach,
Alresford, Hants, SO24 9JH, UK
office1@o-books.net
www.o-books.com

For distributor details and how to order please visit the 'Ordering' section on our website.

Text copyright: Oddvar Olsen 2010

ISBN: 978 1 84694 325 6

All rights reserved. Except for brief quotations in critical articles or reviews, no part of
this book may be reproduced in any manner without prior written permission from
the publishers.

The rights of Oddvar Olsen as author have been asserted in accordance with the Copyright,
Designs and Patents Act 1988.

A CIP catalogue record for this book is available from the British Library.

Design: Tom Davies

Printed in the UK by CPI Antony Rowe
Printed in the USA by Offset Paperback Mfrs, Inc

We operate a distinctive and ethical publishing philosophy in all
areas of our business, from our global network of authors to
production and worldwide distribution.

CONTENTS

List of Plates

Foreword: The Call of the Past
by Sean Martin

The Templars continue to fascinate. Seven hundred years have elapsed since the Order was suppressed, and yet they resolutely refuse to go away. In the popular imagination, they are the guardians of the bloodline of Christ, by way of *The Da Vinci Code* and *The Holy Blood and the Holy Grail*; they are the secret Gnostics of Lawrence Durrell's *Avignon Quintet* and, of course, the villains in Walter Scott's *Ivanhoe*. Before Scott, Renaissance scholars and church historians argued over whether members of the Order of the Poor Knights of Christ and the Temple of Solomon - to give the Order its full title - were saints or sinners. The great antiquarian, scholar and founder member of the Royal Society, Elias Ashmole, looked on the Templars as being 'the principal Columns which supported the Kingdom of Jerusalem' and declared that 'their wealth was their greatest crime'.[1] The official historians of France, the Dupuy brothers, wrote in defence of the Templars' nemesis, the French king Philip IV, and published original trial documents in 1654 to back up their claims that the Templars were indeed guilty as charged. Before the Depuys, the great sixteenth century political theorist Jean Bodin believed the Templars to have been unjustly persecuted, largely innocent victims of the Machiavellian machinations of the church and the French crown. And before Bodin, there was Cornelius Agrippa, who famously declared that the Templars had committed 'detestable heresy'.

Heinrich Cornelius Agrippa von Nettesheim occupies a position in history similar to that of the Templars. Although a Renaissance Humanist scholar, he acquired the reputation of a necromancer and magus, and wrote the most influential magical treatise of his time, *De occulta philosophia*.[2] The book argues that there are two kinds of magic, a base (what has inappropriately been termed 'black') magic and higher form, natural (or 'white') magic, which he terms 'a good and holy science'. Fearful of a backlash, Agrippa chose not to publish the book for over twenty years; it finally appeared in print in 1531. Perhaps he assumed it was safe to do so: after all, he had recently written *Dehortatio gentilis theologiae* (*Against Pagan Theology*) and *De incertitudine et vanitate scientiarum declamatio invectiva* (*On the Uncertainty and Vanity of the Sciences and Arts*), both of which championed adherence to Christian orthodoxy. Despite the apparent Christian piety displayed in these works, Agrippa's plan failed: uproar ensued, and Agrippa quickly published *An Apology* in an attempt to restore his reputation as a respectable scholar. But by then it was too late: he was to be forever cast as the sorcerer, the itinerant wizard accompanied by his sinister familiar, a black dog called Monsieur, and was possibly one of the inspirations for both Marlowe's Dr Faustus and Goethe's Faust.

Why did Agrippa mention the Templars in *De occulta*? He was probably reflecting two centuries of oral tradition about the Order, but his assertion that they held orgies and practised and child sacrifice smacks more of popular superstition than knowledge of a genuine underground Templar tradition. Such charges were famously levelled against the witches, the Jews and the great dualist heretics of the Middle Ages, the Bogomils and the Cathars, and it is ironic that Agrippa should have mentioned the Order at all, given that he himself was precariously close to being arrested for his own 'detestable heresies'. The church never caught up with Agrippa, and he died a free, but poor and obscure, man in 1535.

Before Agrippa, we have the likes of Dante and Boccaccio, both of whom believed the Templars innocent, and Dante's contemporary, Ramon Lull, who believed them to be guilty. He had personally met Jacques de Molay at the time when the Templars were attempting to mount a fresh – and, as it turned out, final - assault on the Holy Land. The failure of the campaign and the loss of the Templar garrison on the island of Ruad, which fell in 1302, must surely have been a disappointment for both de Molay and Lull, both of whom supported the idea of a new, full-scale crusade. Perhaps Lull's disappointment fuelled his belief that the Templars were guilty and his wish to see them punished.

We can carry the thread back further: Pope Innocent III accused the Order of necromancy in 1207, while various Western commentators saw the failure of the Second Crusade as being the result of the treachery of the Templars, who were secretly in league with the Infidel.[3] Going back even further, to the time of the Order's official launch in the West at the Council of Troyes in 1129, we have detractors labelling the Order 'a certain new monster'[4] – an unheard-of cross between a monk and a knight, which was surely unchristian. And the Council members themselves advised the Templars to drop certain practices 'described as absurd'.[5] Even here, this early in the Templars' history, we are on uncertain ground: what were these practices? Were they deviating from church orthodoxy merely in letter, or was it something a little more serious?

The early years of the Order are indeed the stuff of legend, simply because very little survives by way of documentation. Only a handful of records survive, and none of them mention the Templars as protecting pilgrims, the traditional explanation given for the formation of the Order. Even late Templars themselves didn't know exactly why the Order had been founded, and merely repeated the pilgrim-protecting story to Philip IV's inquisitors. There are the persistent stories of the Templars excavating under the Temple Mount and finding something, perhaps by accident during building works, but possibly also because they believed in the stories of the fabulous wealth of Solomon's original temple. That the Order, originally based near the Church of the Holy Sepulchre, had asked Baldwin II, the King of Jerusalem, for quarters on the Temple Platform does indeed suggest that the Order itself was susceptible to the power of myth. The stunning success of the Templars in their early years lends weight to the romance of Solomon's Temple: maybe the Templars did find something, but even if they did not, being based on such a legendary site may have made them feel special – part of a chain of wisdom and righteousness stretching back to Old Testament times.

Whatever part of the Templar story we care to examine, we usually find a disparity between the history of academic writers and the theories of those in more speculative camps. But we must remind ourselves that the mediaeval imagination drew no distinction between history and myth: the fabric of reality itself was one infinitely vast, terrifying but also divinely ordered and therefore beautiful whole. So stories that the Templars possessed the Grail or the Shroud of Turin, or were in fact in league with Islam, were taken at face value. It is of course ironic that new research by academics such as Dr Barbara Frale[6] suggests that the Templars did indeed possess the Turin Shroud: history seems to be finally vindicating some of the myths.

Perhaps the mediaeval worldview, which saw no difference between history and myth, is more enriching, more *human*, for want of a better word, than the modern tendency to rationalise and analyse. The Middle Ages might have been the era in which life was 'nasty, brutish and short', to quote Thomas Hobbes, centuries of plague and infant mortality, but it was also an age of faith, of the great cathedrals, of the Troubadours and poets. We, meanwhile, have all the comforts of life in the 21st century, and can expect a reasonable lifespan, but the price has been steep: we live in a culture in which the imagination has atrophied, and if the word is used at all , it is in the pejorative sense. Worse, we have, collectively, lost our soul.

It is perhaps in exploring the apparent dichotomies between History/Myth and Mediaeval/Modern that we can perhaps begin to recover the soul. Academic historians may scoff, but when there is no clear agreement between them – such as in the case of whether de Molay uttered his famous 'curse' from the pyre (some say he did, while others believe he did not) – the whole notion of a more inclusive, well-informed but speculative approach to the Templars, becomes a more attractive, and perhaps necessary, proposition. Indeed, it takes us closer to the more traditional world-view that the mediaevals knew, a double vision that, as Patrick Harpur notes, 'does not lead to some final solution, some absolute truth; it is itself truth. We are transformed by the Way we take... which has no end in this world, nor even perhaps in the next.'[7]

It is such speculation and exploration that the various writers in *Temple Antiquities - The Templar Papers 2* offer us: from the enigmatic Templar heads and green men to the Order's activities in Scotland and central Europe. But, as the other papers in the present volume suggest, covering as they do diverse topics such as Shakespeare, Poussin and faery traditions, why stop at the Templars? As Emerson said, 'broader and deeper we must write our annals'[8] and it is in these broad, deep strokes that we can begin to recover, if not something of the past, then perhaps a version of it that is valid for the time in which it is being written, a mirror in which we may see ourselves more clearly. Perhaps we might also recover something of our own imaginations, of ourselves. And possibly even a tentative, mercurial, sliver of soul.

Sean Martin
Somerset
June 2009

1   Quoted in Peter Partner, *The Knights Templar and their Myth*, (Rochester, VT: Inner Traditions, 1990), p. 97

2   Available in English as *Three Books of Occult Philosophy* (St Paul, MN: Llewellyn Publications, 1997).

3   Such as the two Würzburg chroniclers, the monk John and his anonymous colleague, known as the Würzburg Annalist. Later chronicles, such as that by Bernard and Ernoul the Treasurer, written in the thirteenth century, have the Hospitallers acting in treacherous league with the Templars.

4   The phrase is Henry of Huntingdon's (*c*. 1080-1160).

5   Malcolm Barber, *The Trial of the Templars* (Cambridge: Cambridge University Press, Second Edition, 2006) p. 8

6   'Knights Templar hid the Shroud of Turin, says Vatican', *The Times*, 6 April 2009.

7   Patrick Harpur, *Daimonic Reality: A Field Guide to the Otherworld* (London: Viking Arkana, 1994), p.254

8   Ralph Waldo Emerson, 'History', *Nature and Selected Essays* (Harmondsworth: Penguin Classics, 2003)

Chapter 1

Perceval's Grail Quest as Redemption of the Sacred Feminine
By Forrest D. Lamb

Over the past millennia, the tales of King Arthur have become the most well known and best loved of all European mythologies, with the Grail cycles specifically becoming the focus of widespread spiritual/mystical/esoteric interest. The Quest for the Holy Grail is widely understood to be the search for spiritual perfection; the yearning after communion with God, of total enlightenment and complete knowledge. Chretien de Troyes' *Perceval (or Le Conte du Graal)* is the first written example that we have which describes a specifically Christo-Arthurian based context for this Quest.[1] The Grail has been represented and interpreted in various ways over the centuries and to this day it continues to be a source of fascination for many.[2] This article will examine Chretien's *Le Conte du Graal*, and in so doing, demonstrate that the story's quest for spiritual perfection can be seen as a reconciliation of the feminine principle, a re-discovery of the Goddess, with the dominant patriarchal nature of Western Christianity.

Although Perceval is the first written Grail story, it was the last of Chretien's works. His previous tales, or romances, were all placed to some degree within the periphery of King Arthur's court, and while they appear to be set in the timeframe of the historical Arthur (circa 5th-6th century), the courts which Chretien described were accurate emulations of the courts which existed in the 12th century, and which he was believed to have moved within. [3] Not only did Chretien provide us with *Perceval*, the first example we have of the modern Grail story, but he can also be credited for the modern notion of romance, [4] the first time we are presented with what we would today recognise as chivalry.

Prior to Chretien, the notion of chivalry was confined to the tenets, practicalities and etiquettes of war, as well as the knights' favourite pastime, the tournament. To this, however, Chretien attached, for the first time, the fundamental importance of courtly love. In Chretien's eyes, the adoration and honouring of ladies was the *raison d'etre*, the foundation, for all of chivalry's practicalities. This emphasis upon love and its pursuit, 'this *fin amor* as it was called, was revolutionary...It defied Church and society by giving woman a higher status and superior worth to man's.' But where had this defiance come from? Chretien's era was concurrent with the great troubadour movement of the Occitan; the region which boasted fervent goddess cults, dedicated to the likes of Mary Magdalene, Diana, Isis, the Queen of Heaven, etc. The Occitan was home to the Cathars, a Dualist/Gnostic Christian movement, which just happened to be much more tolerant of females generally, and within religion specifically. These beliefs, through the poems of the troubadours and contact through the crusades, would gradually encounter the militarily efficient Northern Franks, and this synthesis of the Gentlemanly Honour of the Warrior Caste with the Noble Love of the Troubadours, would germinate in the first romance novels. The pre-eminent of these, and the first example we have is Chretien's *Le Conte du Graal*, which introduced the world to 'the religion of love which for about a century had gradually spread through the literary circles of southern France.'[5]

All of Chretien's works deal specifically with the idea of romantic love, irrevocably intertwined with the glory and pitfalls of chivalric adventure. We can also gather that the specific idea of noble love, love untarnished by immorality, was an important concern for Chretien, as we know he conspicuously avoided the morally tenuous legends of Lancelot and Guinevere, and Tristan and Isolde.[6] But what really seemed to interest Chretien was the tension between doing what one knows to be morally correct and doing what one's heart insists upon. As Richard Barber, an eminent Arthurian scholar, points out, 'His favourite study is love in all its moods,' noting further, 'his focal point is the realistic depiction of characters and the study of love – all his romances have as central figures a hero and heroine, except perhaps the last.' This last, which Barber refers to, is *Perceval*, the initial Grail story which remained ultimately unfinished, due, it is believed to Chretien's untimely death.

In reply to Barber's conclusion, I would argue here that *all* of Chretien's stories can be interpreted as that development of individual character, through their moral choice and via the honourable, dedicated pursuit of Love. The difference in the case of Perceval, and the foundation of my argument, is that Perceval is also a potent love story, the *ultimate* love story in fact, the *hieros gamos* (sacred marriage) of god and goddess, epicentre of perfect balance and wisdom; the all-consuming desire to submit the power of one's masculinity to the needs of the Holy Mother. In *Le Conte du Graal*, therefore, this interpretation will examine the salvation of man, as well as the salvation of Man's Kingdom (the Wasteland), through his active redemption of the Feminine; thus the Quest for the Holy Grail, the quest for spiritual reunion, a perfection which can be understood as the rebalancing of the divine energies, Feminine and Masculine. *Perceval* is assuredly a love story, the knight's Desire for Love, in a world where patri-archal dominance has resulted in a Wasteland, one which can only be healed through the recovery of the Goddess.

Becoming a Knight

'Have I not just seen the most beautiful things there are, going through the Waste Forest? They are more beautiful, I think, than God or all his angels...They say they are called knights.'

The story of Perceval is the story of the innocent, entering the world in ignorance, with little to guide him but the sheltering words of his mother; an obvious metaphor of the child's journey into adulthood. In the case of Perceval, he lives alone with his mother in the safety of the Waste Forest, far from the dangers and the splendours of the 'real world.' Unbeknownst to Perceval, the reason behind this lies in the fact that his mother is hiding him out of fear for his safety; his father, a pre-eminent knight, had been mortally wounded and died upon hearing of the deaths of his two elder sons, who were also killed in knightly combat. His mother fears terribly that Perceval will succumb to a similar fate because of this the very last thing that she wishes is that he will one day become a knight. Of course fate has other plans for the both of them.

One day while in the Forest hunting, Perceval (who has come to be known by later scholars as the Perfect Fool) comes upon a group of men on horses, first mistaking them for demons due to their clamour, and next for angels due to their splendour; they are in fact a group of knights in pursuit of Arthur, their liege. After questioning the knights, and in the process demonstrating his complete ignorance by the banality of his queries, he decides there and then that he too will become a knight and that there is nothing in this world that will stop him from doing so. The stage is now set for Perceval's adventures to begin and for his mother's fears to come true.

It is here, as Chretien's love story begins to germinate, that the important ideas of the mother, of the story as a metaphor for the redemption of the Goddess can first be discerned. Chretien refers to Perceval, who is unaware of his own name, as the 'son of the widow.' The fact that scholars routinely ignore this designation is confounding. The *son of the widow* is a blatant signpost, an ancient title that has been used in conjunction with several prominent gods and historical figures; these gods include Horus, son of Isis and the deceased Osiris, and Tammuz, *son of the widow* of Nimrod, and more pertinently, Jesus himself was called *son of the widow* by the self-proclaimed prophet Mani, founder of the Manichean movement; he also considered himself a *son of the widow*, the adopted slave son of a Roman widow. As an example of the lasting power of this title, the Masonic Temple has subsequently used it for centuries to describe Hiram Abif, their mythological founder. The use of the *widow's son* title by Chretien is infrequently mentioned, but always so that it can be claimed that Perceval is analogous to a Christ-figure.

For the purpose of my argument, what is so interesting about the *son of the widow*, is the *widow*. If Perceval can be equated with Horus, Tammuz, Mani and Jesus, then, moreover, his mother needs be equated with the goddess! When this connection is considered closely, so many of Chretien's strange episodes and seemingly random connections in *Le Conte du Graal* are thrown into sharper relief. If nothing else, it is much easier to focus upon Perceval's relationship with his mother and how it literally dominates the story from start to finish.

Elaborating upon the emphasis of Perceval's relationship with his mother, from a well-presented Jungian perspective, is the seminal work, *The Grail Legend* by Emma Jung and Marie-Louise von Franz. Jung and von Franz' book is a study of the archetypes represented in the Grail cycles using Chretien's work as its primary model. According to *The Grail Legend*, the Waste Forest itself is a perfect representation of the maternal figure in the innocence's life, 'Understood as protecting and nourishing nature, the forest also represents the all-embracing quality of the mother,' and further, 'This primitive state is emphasised by the fact that Perceval is fatherless and knows only his mother, who brings him up in loneliness, far from the world.'[7] For Jung and von Franz, the relationship that Perceval has with his mother is the central theme of the story, and therefore the archetype of the mother is the key to any true understanding of its psychological import;

> This leads us to a consideration of the transpersonal significance of the mother. From this angle she is not so much a particular person as she is the absolutely universal giver and preserver of life, and as such she may be compared to the unconscious which is the source and origin of all psychic life.[8]

The combination of the boy's mother, with the womblike surroundings of the Waste Forest, isolate him completely; he simply knows nothing other than what his mother tells him, and how to hunt within their wood. Informing his mother that he intends to leave the forest to become a knight, she of course, begs him not to leave, but seeing his resolve, tells him the true story of his father and of his brothers, desperately hoping that Perceval will show her compassion. But he is simply incapable at this point of anything but selfishness,

> The boy paid scarcely any attention to what his mother said, 'Give me something to eat,' he said. 'I don't understand your words, but I would gladly go to the king whom makes knights; and I will go no matter what.' [9]

Discomforted, she ceases her attempts to dissuade him and instead gives him some motherly wisdom, simple rules which he must abide by out in the world. Her first request is that he help all ladies and maidens in need and to assist them if they ask him it of him, for, 'He who fails to honour ladies finds his own honour dead inside him. Serve ladies and maidens and you will be honoured everywhere.' [10]

The widow proceeds, telling him, 'And if you ask any for her love, be careful not to annoy her by doing anything to displease her. He who kisses a maiden gains much, but if she grants you a kiss, I forbid you to go any further, if you'll refrain for my sake.'[11] So, having given her son her unwilling blessings to leave her in the Forest, she additionally instructs him, if he really loves her, not to have any sexual relationship with another woman! This simple request by the widow, which it appears that Perceval acquiesces to over the course of the narrative, immediately delineates all of the knight's relationships with women to be interpreted idealistically, not literally. With the sexual tension released from his female encounters, they take on airs of truly noble love, the desire to right what is wrong with every gentle lady he comes across. Perceval's mother has set the tone and clearly defined for him the nature of his quests, the vigilant redemption of the feminine divine.

Of course, Perceval agrees quickly and without thinking, to these, as well as her other requests and decides to leave their home in all haste. As he leaves astride his horse, he turns one last time to look at her, but she 'had fallen at the head of the bridge and was lying in a faint as if she had dropped dead.'[12] Again, being not an inkling of compassion within Perceval yet, he simply doesn't react to the sight of his fallen mother, and proceeds out into the world to become a knight. These episodes clearly demonstrate the intensity of the relationship between the widow and her son, and foreshadow the issues which Perceval will struggle with for the balance of the narrative.

To emphasise the importance of Perceval's relationships with women to the narrative, Chretien gives to him, as his first challenge outside of the Waste Forest, neither a battle nor a feat of courage, but a lone maiden, asleep and vulnerable. In a meadow, Perceval comes across what he believes is a magnificent church (though in reality it's a tent) and enters it to pray, as his mother had instructed him to do. Within the tent, he finds a maiden alone and asleep on her bed, and here shows that he had not at all heard nor understood what his mother had instructed him to do. As he steps into the tent, the maiden awakens and begs him to leave, informing him that her master will return shortly and will surely kill him if he sees Perceval in the tent; to which he replies,

> 'First I'll kiss you, by my head,' said the boy, ''no matter what anyone may think, because my mother instructed me to.' [13]

And having kissed her against her will 'twenty times as the story says', he spots a ring on her finger, saying:

> 'My mother also told me,' he said, 'to take the ring from your finger, but not to do anything more. Now give me the ring; I want it!' [14]

The insolent, self-centred Perceval takes the ring by force, even as she begs him not to, saying she'll be treated badly because of it, and finally eats and drinks the provisions he finds in the tent. Though he has set out from the Waste Forest to become an honourable knight, and despite his mother's clear instructions about honouring women and not displeasing them, his first act on the road to masculine glory is to disgrace a maiden; an act which will result in dreadful hardship and humiliation for the young lady, as we are to learn later in the story. It is indeed interesting that even before Perceval has a chance to prove his strength and courage, he fails his first challenge. Perceval's failure to understand instruction and thus, his certain failure at treating the maiden with honour, is a perfect foreshadowing of the knight's destined failure in the castle of the Fisher King. Outside of the Waste Forest, having broken his mother's heart with his first act of free will and dishonoured a fair maiden with his desires and ignorance with the second, the redemption of women will subsequently figure prominently in each of the young knight's adventures; it is plainly the central theme, one which Chretien will bring us back to time and again.

Perceval's next move is to make his way to Carlisle, to find King Arthur and to have himself made into a knight. Outside the gates of the castle, Perceval meets the Red Knight, who informs the boy that the king refuses to pay homage to him for his lands and therefore he has insisted upon a duel with one of his knights, and in addition he has audaciously stolen a golden cup from Arthur's hand, with his wine still inside. Perceval ignores all of this and heads for the castle to be knighted, all the while coveting the magnificent armour of the Red Knight, but there is a problem. When Perceval uncouthly rides his horse right into Arthur's court, the king is still downcast, the Red Knight has spilt wine all over the queen and as done him and her a grave dishonour. So, downcast is the king, that he does not acknowledge Perceval's presence, until the uncouth lad accidentally knocks his cap from his head with his mount.

During this episode, the importance of the redemption of the lady is again critical to an understanding of the sequence of events. It can be argued that, what should have been causing Arthur's grief was that the Red Knight had upstaged him, or that his authority over his lands had been challenged and, perhaps most painfully, that none of his famous knights had taken up the challenge on his behalf (as specifically requested by the Red Knight). However, what is actually causing him grief is that his golden cup had been stolen and that in the process, his queen had been sullied by the wine flying from it. The golden cup is an important aspect of this scene; the cup is an ancient symbol of the feminine principal, mirroring the womb, and the wine a universal symbol of blood. Therefore, the figure of Man's greatest physical strength, King Arthur, is grieved most bitterly and debilitated to distraction, by the loss of his symbol of the feminine (the cup) and the loss of his wife's presence, who is so angry that she leaves, stained with the 'blood' of his weakness, as Arthur explains to Perceval,

> *The knight would never have angered me by words alone, but he snatched away my cup and lifted it so insolently that he spilled all the wine in it over the queen. After this dreadful deed the queen returned to her chambers, in deadly fury and grief. So help me God, I don't think she'll come out alive.*[15]

Perceval, still in the role as the Fool, takes no heed of the king's problems and insists that Arthur make him a knight then and there. Before Arthur has the chance, the boy becomes impatient, demands the armour of the Red Knight (which Arthur's seneschal Kay insolently tells him to go and take) and prepares to leave. Before he can do so, a maiden in the court sees Perceval, laughs joyfully and says to him 'Young man, if you live long enough, I think and believe in my heart that in this whole world there will never be, nor will anyone ever acknowledge, a better knight than yourself. This I think and feel and believe.'[16] Hearing this Kay jumps up and slaps the maiden in the face angrily, then turns and kicks a jester into the fire, because, as Chretien tells us, the jester had often said that, 'This maiden will not laugh until she has seen the man who will be the supreme lord among all knights.'[17]

Having left the Waste Forest, and his fallen mother, to find the mighty King Arthur and to become a knight, Perceval finds instead a dismally incapacitated figure, stricken by his inability to protect the honour of his queen, and because of this, the boy actually gains his first validation from an unknown maiden, who foretells of his greatness. Chretien chooses a handmaiden of the queen's to announce Perceval's destiny, despite the presence of the king and the other knights; Perceval is empowered and guided at every crucial event by a noble woman. The fact that he confronts and kills the Red Knight, the king's mortal enemy, while Arthur is incapable of any response at all, additionally removes the stain upon the queen's honour; his first official victory for the Lady. Throughout the remainder of the story, he never forgets the young maiden's encouragement, dedicating victory after victory to this unknown lady's honour.

The final step in Perceval's path to becoming a knight is his chance meeting with a gentleman called Gornemant of Gohort. Gornemant himself is of no great interest in the tale other than he quickly teaches Perceval to ride and to fight properly, and by his instruction and through the performing of customs, officially makes Perceval a knight by attaching a spur to his right boot. However, one of the pieces of advice which Gornemant gives to Perceval does contribute significantly to the narrative. The vavasour tells the young knight that he should refrain from talking too much, as doing so is considered a sin by wise men. This simple advice will inevitably cause Perceval's greatest failure, Gornemant's influence upon the knight, especially as the only significant male role model Perceval finds, is significant, for hidden in his practical advise are the seeds of Perceval's great failure.

Becoming a Man

'Friend, if your heart is in it,' said the gentleman, 'you'll learn much and never experience any difficulty.'

Perceval's transformation from the ignorant Welshman to supreme knight becomes reality at the castle of Biaurepaire. Having left Gornemant in search of his fallen mother, the knight comes upon a troubled castle, besieged as it is, there is little in the way of provision or ceremony for the new knight. The lady of the castle, Blancheflor, with apologies, invites Perceval to lodge with them and receive what comforts they can manage. A quiet meal and conversation leads the two into each other's arms that very night, and before long Blancheflor is bemoaning her castle's condition; simultaneously refusing Perceval's sympathies, while secretly desiring for him to fight on her behalf. In the morning, she accepts the chaste knight's decision to defend her castle and her honour, and she, in turn, declares that her heart belongs to him eternally if he is successful.

The ensuing victories over Blancheflor's besiegers, and the blossoming love between the queen and her defender, gives Perceval his first chance to redeem himself properly as a true knight; the compassion which he shows her, due to their love, due to the realisation that he was not complete without this lady's love, marks the knight's transition from adventurer to quester. Love acts as the gateway to compassion, the move from selfishness to selflessness, and Perceval's passion for Blancheflor awakens this in his consciousness. After defeating Anguingueron and Clamadeu in separate battles, Perceval also shows mercy upon them (as instructed by Gornemant) and sends them both back to Carlisle, in honour of the queen's handmaiden who had been insulted by Kay. In the process of his victories and his actions, Perceval can be said to be a true knight in the eyes of Chretien, one who has acted nobly, acted with compassion and who has brought honour to two different women, as promised.

Upon securing the situation at Biaurepaire, Blancheflor offers the lordship of the castle to Perceval. His beloved is safe and prosperous in her castle, but Perceval cannot accept the invitation; there is a greater quest which he must resume, to return to his mother. Perceval promises to bring his mother back to Biaurepaire if he can find her, but insists on going as quickly as possible, as he now understands the pain of separation. This is the second time (along with Gornemant) that Perceval declares that he must find his mother and determine what her condition is, after the agony that he has knowingly and willingly inflicted upon her. The first time he sets out for his mother, he comes upon Biaurepaire and true love; the second time he departs he will discover something even more captivating: the mystery of the holy grail.

Becoming Perfect: The Quest

> *'But Perceval swore a different oath, saying that he would not spend two nights in the same lodgings as long as he lived...He would not abandon his quest for any hardship.'*

Having said his goodbyes to Blancheflor, Perceval rides until he comes to a great river, which too wide to cross. Seeing a pair of men in a fishing boat, Perceval enquires if they know a means of crossing the broad river. The knight is informed that there is no way to cross for twenty leagues, but that if he requires accommodation for the night, he was welcome to stay as a guest at the gentleman's castle. Perceval gladly accepts the invitation. The gentleman in the boat, the Fisher King, is already present in the castle when Perceval arrives and takes him into his home for conversation and a meal. While they lounge in a great hall talking, a young girl brings the Fisher King a precious sword, telling him that it is a gift of one of his nieces and that he is free to give it to whomever he pleases. He unhesitatingly presents the sword to Perceval. After the food is brought out, Perceval and the Fisher King then witness a strange procession:

> *...a squire came forth from a chamber carrying a white lance by the middle of its shaft; he passed between the fire and those seated upon the bed. Everyone in the hall saw the white lance with its white point from whose tip there issued a drop of blood, and this red drop flowed down to the squire's hand.* [18]

This sight bewilders the young knight, but in deference to Gornemant's advice, he keeps his mouth closed for fear of speaking idly. Following on the heels of the squire and the bleeding lance, two more squires enter the hall carrying a set of golden candelabra each, candles ablaze. The next in line in the procession is perhaps the most important figure in all the stories of the Grail cycle, the Grail maiden;

> *A maiden accompanying the two young men was carrying a grail with her two hands; she was beautiful, noble, and richly attired. After she had entered the hall carrying the grail, the room was so brightly illumined that the candles lost their brilliance like stars and the moon when the sun rises.*[19]

Last in the procession is a maiden carrying a silver carving platter, but Chretien makes little of this final participant. What he does make much of however, is the grail itself. Most scholars agree that in Chretien's use of the word, graal means some sort of platter that fish was generally served upon. Considering the story's continuous references to Christianity, the symbol of the Grail being overtly connected to that of a Fish is hardly surprising. Having watched this event in silence, the king and the knight begin to dine upon the tables of food in front of them and as they eat the Grail procession passes by; again and again in fact, '...with each course that was served he saw the grail pass by completely uncovered before him.' Still, Perceval remains silent and refuses to enquire of the Spear and the Grail, believing that he will ask one of the squires in the morning of what he had witnessed.

After goodnights and a good night's sleep, Perceval awakens to find the castle completely deserted. He calls out and searches the keep, but to no avail and is forced to put on his own armour, to prepare his own horse and to ride out alone. Utterly confused by what has transpired, the knight stops on the drawbridge, turns back one last time to call out to the castle, but as he does so the bridge begins to raise. Perceval and his horse must desperately jump the last few feet to safety across the mote; he has been forcibly shut out of the keep and has lost his chance to find out any answers to his questions. Fortunately, he will not have to wait long to learn most of what has happened to him and to discover his true destiny.

A short ride from the Fisher King's castle, Perceval comes across a weeping maiden alone in the woods, holding a dead, beheaded knight in her arms. She informs Perceval that her beloved had been killed that very morning. But the lady is utterly astonished at the mere presence of Perceval in those woods, according to her there is no castle for twenty-five leagues, yet he looks fresh and well rested. After assuring her that he had stayed close by and had indeed slept well, the maiden deduces that he must have stayed in the castle of the Fisher King; now she is very interested in Perceval's story,

> '..tell me whether you saw the lance with the tip that bleeds, though it has neither blood nor veins.'
> 'Yes, upon my word, I did see it!'
> 'And did you ask why it bled?'
> 'I never spoke a word.'
> 'So help me God, let me tell you then that you have done ill. And did you see the grail?'
> 'Quite clearly.'
> 'Who carried it?'
> 'A maiden.'
> 'Did you ask people where they were going in this manner?'
> 'No question came from my mouth.'
> 'So help me God, now it's even worse!' [20]

The maiden asks the knight's name, and having to guess, tells her that it is Perceval; he has guessed correctly and she knows him instantly. As it happens, the maiden is his cousin and knows him well. She informs him that he has committed a grave error, as he could have healed the Fisher King and the Wasteland simultaneously, had he only inquired about all he had seen. Additionally, she tells him that the reason that he has failed in this endeavour is because he has sinned against his mother, who his cousin now confirms actually died that day Perceval saw her collapsed on the bridge. Tellingly, the maiden is as distraught over Perceval's failure in the Fisher King's castle as she is over the death of his mother, or the dead lover she holds in her arms. Although compassion has entered into the knight's consciousness, symbolised by the gift of the fragile sword,[21] his reaction to the news still reveals a lack of true depth, 'You've brought me terrible news. And since she's buried in the ground what reason do I have to continue onwards, for I had set off only because I wished to see her again? I must change my course...'[22]

His cousin directs him to take a nearby cobbled road, which he takes, and after a short while he comes upon a girl in rags, riding a broken down, ill-treated horse. She urges him to ride on before her tormentor appears and kills him, but as they speak a black knight rides toward them and condemns Perceval for delaying the miserable girl. Before he attacks however, he insists upon telling Perceval the story of the girl and why he keeps her in tatters; the story of the maiden in the tent, except that he believes the girl must have given into the Welsh boy completely, relinquishing her ring and her chastity in the process. Perceval replies that the maiden has served her penance in full, because it was he who had taken the ring and the kisses, but nothing more than these, his pies and his wine. The Haughty Knight of the Heath becomes enraged at this admission, and attacks Perceval, however, he is no match for the knight supreme. Again, Perceval shows mercy to his defeated adversary and directs the knight to take the maiden and himself to Arthur's court, giving his sword to the king's service, while the maiden was given over to the queen.

This sequence of events, with Perceval's cousin and with the Haughty Knight of the Heath, continue Chretien's emphasis upon the redemption of the feminine as the noblest cause, as well as highlighting the female's ultimate soteriological importance. Upon hearing of the death of his mother, Perceval's first great quest is over; there is now no chance of finding his mother or bringing her succour. During the course of his quest for his mother, however, Perceval has acted as redeemer to Arthur's queen for the dishonour she suffered, acted as noble hero and saviour to Blancheflor, has found true love in the process, and has redeemed both his cousin and the maiden in the tent, through his defeat of the Haughty Knight. As mentioned previously, these women are also responsible for launching the knight on his travels; Perceval's lack of compassion for his mother at the beginning of the story results in his primary quest of returning to her, and now his cousin informs him that it was indeed that same act, his sin against his mother, along with his lack of compassion for the Fisher King's plight, which will direct him towards his true quest.

At this point in the story, much of Perceval's adventuring has been concluded. The Haughty Knight takes the maiden to Arthur's court, as commanded, and pledges himself to the king's service. The king, seeing such an impressive knight before him, knows that it must surely be Perceval who has sent him, and declares there and then that he will not sleep two nights in the same place until he can find the knight. Having left Carlisle, the king's court almost instantly comes upon Perceval, reflecting in silence upon the beauty of his beloved, Blancheflor, while staring at three drops of blood in the snow. Two knights come out and, not knowing it is him that Arthur seeks, try to force him into the camp. In his fury at being distracted from his contemplations, he knocks both men from their horses, the second of them being Kay, who upon landing in the snow, breaks his arm. The jester's prophecy comes true and the laughing maiden is at last completely avenged of Kay's vicious slap.

After spending a few days of rest and relaxation with Arthur and his court, and upon making his only friend of the narrative, Gawain, there came into the midst of the camp a Hideous Maiden, who brings tidings from the surrounding countryside and news of a tournament where all the fame and fortune a knight could want can be gained. Upon seeing Perceval, however, she cries out,

Ah, Perceval! Fortune is bald behind and hairy in front. Cursed be anyone who'd greet you or who'd wish you well, for you didn't catch hold of Fortune when you met her! You entered the castle of the Fisher King and saw the bleeding lance, but it was so much effort for you to open your mouth and speak that you couldn't ask why that drop of blood flowed from the tip of the white shaft! And you didn't ask or inquire what rich man was served from the grail you saw. Wretched is the man who sees that the propitious hour has come but waits for a still better one.[23]

The Hideous Maiden continues to berate Perceval for his timidity and his ignorance, telling all that were listening of the catastrophes which would occur because of him; women losing husbands, lands laid waste, maidens left unprotected and many knights dead. Chretien again guides Perceval along his path by the heralding of a maiden; they become signposts for the knight's destiny, they act as mirrors for his morality, markers of his progress, and the means by which he is empowered to continue upon his quests. This time, the Hideous Maiden refers specifically to the quest which he has failed; having seen Fortune (or Lady Luck, or Providence, the feminine divine nature of prosperity) right in front of him, he lets her pass by freely. The feminine principal being professed by Chretien is the source of all goodness, the wellspring from which love, consciousness and wisdom flow. Under the guise of the Hideous Maiden, the goddess is a representation of despair, a symbol of loss, pain and death; she has now been seen in her traditionally pagan triple aspects of mother, maiden (Blancheflor) and crone (Hideous Maiden). And all three have sent him upon separate, but intimately related, quests. Firstly, Perceval leaves his mother in search of the Self, secondly, he leaves Blancheflor in search of Consciousness, and lastly, Perceval will depart from Arthur's court upon hearing the Hideous Maiden's denouncement, on the quest for total redemption and personal salvation.

Although King Arthur and his entire court of knights had also hear the ominous words of the Hideous Maiden, not one of them entertain for a second the notion of going with Perceval, nor helping him in any way. Instead, they head off, practically *en masse*, to the tournament she has announced, wherefrom fame and fortune beckoned to them. Unlike later Grail stories, such as *Parzifal* and the *High History of the Holy Grail*, Perceval here, is alone on his quest to find the secret of the grail and the bleeding lance. As it has been from the beginning, Chretien's Perceval narrative is the journey of the individual, on the path from naivety and ignorance, to love and compassion, through to wisdom and enlightenment. Just as he alone was responsible for the redemption of all those along his journey, the redemption of the Fisher King and of the Wasteland will also fall solely upon Perceval's shoulders. Now, having the consciousness of love and of pain, in addition to the clarity of what he has done and what he must do, the knight officially announces his quest,

> But Perceval swore a different oath, saying that he would not spend two nights in the same lodgings as long as he lived, nor hear word of any dangerous passage that he would not go to cross, nor learn of a knight of pre-eminent repute, or even two, that would not test himself against, until he had learned who was served from the grail and had found the bleeding lance and been told the true reason why it bled. He would not abandon his hardship for any reason.[24]

As I mentioned earlier, as far as the narrative is concerned,

Perceval's questing and adventuring are finished. Chretien tells us that, 'as the story is told,' Perceval so completely loses his memory that he forgets not only his pledge to return to Blancheflor, but himself, his quest and indeed God. In the five years that follow, Perceval wanders in a complete 'cloud of unknowing,' continuing in pursuit of chivalric acts, defeating sixty knights in that time and sending them to Arthur's service. But his sense of purpose and his knowledge of self are lost, he goes through the motions of his previous life with no joy, nor sense of accomplishment. This condition continues until he comes across a group of knights and ladies, who chastise him for wearing full armour on Good Friday; Perceval literally does not know what day it is, and after the group affirm for him that this is indeed the day that Jesus Christ died, Perceval is finally shaken out of his miasma and was 'troubled in his heart that he had no idea of the day or the hour or the time.'[25]

The group inform him that they have been to see the local hermit and that he should go and confess his sins to him. Perceval weeps at the remembrance of God and his neglect of worship during the five-year fog, pledging to seek him out if they will only point him in the right direction. Finding the hermit in a nearby chapel, Perceval begs him for absolution of his sins, which the hermit agrees to, if he will confess and repent of his sins. The knight recounts the events of the past five years and his forgetting of God, which prompts the hermit to ask for the cause of this unknowing, Perceval replies,

> *Sir, I was once at the manor of the Fisher King, and I saw the lance whose point bleeds beyond doubt, and I never asked about this drop of blood I saw suspended from the white iron tip. I've done nothing since then to make amends, and I never learned who was served from the grail I saw.*[26]

With this, the hermit-priest asks his name, which Perceval gives him. With a sigh at the sound, the hermit informs him (as his cousin had) that the cause of his failure at the Fisher King's castle is due to his sinning against his mother. Additionally, and crucially, the hermit declares that without the continuing love of his mother, even after death, he could have achieved nothing, 'And understand that you would not have lasted until now had she not commended you to God; but her prayer was so powerful that God watched over you for her sake and kept you from death and imprisonment.'[27]

In turn, the hermit also reveals that he himself is the brother of the one who is served from the grail and a brother of Perceval's own mother; the hermit is the knight's uncle and the Fisher King his first cousin. Here, the hermit at last divulges a secret of the Grail procession, namely that the father of the Fisher King is sustained solely by a single host, which is served to him from the Grail daily. Finishing the strange tale of the Grail, the hermit-priest imposes proper penitence upon Perceval for his sins; the knight must visit a chapel everyday to repent, before he visits anywhere else, thus focusing his full intent and purpose on God, 'Believe in God, love God worship God; *honour gentlemen and noble ladies*, arise in the presence of the priest.'[28] (another small allusion to honouring the male and the female equally) The final steps of Perceval's penitence are receiving a list of God's true names ('which should never be uttered by the mouth of man except in peril of death') and to remain with his uncle at the chapel for two days, eating only what the old man eats. On Easter Sunday, Perceval speaks an oath to his belief of Jesus Christ and receives communion.

This is the last which we hear of Perceval in Le Conte du Graal, excepting the several later continuations of Chretien's original; we cannot know if he ever finds the grail, nor if he discovers the true cause of the bleeding lance, or if he returns to Blancheflor as promised. Given the lack of resolution to much of the tension in the story, it is somewhat surprising that Chretien's original version has had such an impact on the study of the Grail cycles. However, the lack of ending positively accentuates the story's main insight or wisdom; that it is in the journey itself, that the transformation from innocence to wisdom, from the periphery of one's own soul to the centre, from selfish love to selfless love, take place. These are the journeys we must make as individuals, developing as we walk along our paths, gaining knowledge and perspective. It is therefore the process of searching for one's highest calling, not necessarily the attainment of the goal, which is the true wisdom of the mystery of the grail. And for Chretien's hero, Perceval, that highest calling was nothing less than the pursuit of spiritual perfection, a Quest which was given to him and defined for him, by the women he encounters, and for whom every victory is dedicated.

Conclusion: The Goddess and The Grail

If it can be shown clearly that the structure of *Le Conte du Graal* has been systematically formulated to revolve around the redemption of the feminine principal, then it can also be demonstrated that there are many events in the narrative which act as portents, clues obstructed by Chretien's ingenious use of foreshadowing. The examples are numerous; Perceval's failure to recognise the extent of his fallen mother's illness, results in the story's secondary quest, the search for his mother and the ultimate realisation that she is lost. This is a perfect prefiguring of the knight's failure to recognise his destiny when it arrives at the Fisher King's castle, because of this failure, Perceval will again be sent spiralling out upon a quest, one which will also remain unfulfilled. The quest for the mother is the quest for the grail, the quest for reunion, completion, perfect balance, and perfect harmony.

The presence of the deeply pagan goddess trinity (maiden, mother, crone) can be no accident; it is via these female forces that the knight learns all of his spiritual lessons. Gornemant may shine the armour, but all of Perceval's concepts of goodness, compassion and love are given him by the softly changing aspects of Chretien's female characters; characters who all seem strikingly similar. It is at this point that the poet's emphasis upon *Eros* becomes most apparent. Having, in effect, neutered Perceval in the Waste Forest, through his mother's strange request for his celibacy, the love that the knight ends up displaying is a clear, passionate and noble love, which itself is a reflection of the purity displayed by the women who evoke it. This is the love for the Goddess, the ultimate Ideal of unrequited love, of passionate love; here it is the quest to redeem one's self, through submission to the feminine divine.

In Julius Evola's *The Mystery of the Grail*, he describes brilliantly the importance of finding a balance between the noble qualities of man and the beautiful qualities of woman, and how this integration is the pathway to perfection,

> *First of all, it is necessary to show the proof and the confirmation of the virile qualification; thus in the epic and knightly symbolism we find a series of adventures, feats and fights…Second, such liberation should not signify a cessation of the inner tension…The consequence of this is the Olympian transformation or the achievement of that dignity which in initiatory traditions has always been signified as "regal." This is the decisive point that differentiates the heroic experience from every mystical evasion and from every pantheistic confusion; among the various symbols that may refer to this point is the symbolism of the woman.*[29]

This is an excellent description of the process of reintegration and how it relates specifically to the pursuit of spiritual perfection within the heroic saga. There are important symbolic representations within Perceval which portray this process of healing the Masculine principle through the love of the Feminine. Nowhere is this clearer than in the grail procession itself. I don't think that it can be overemphasised that the physical grail does not play the lead role in Chretien's narrative; as mentioned above, Perceval doesn't even remember that he's looking for the Grail after he is specifically sets out on his quest. In fact, the grail itself is only mentioned on a handful of occasions and is always mentioned in conjunction with another item that, if the narrative is to be judged, is every bit as important as its more conspicuous counterpart.

Our first introduction to the Grail is in the castle of the Fisher King and it is here where we would expect the Holy Relic to take centre stage, but it doesn't. After all, during the course of Perceval's evening with the Fisher King, the 'Grail procession' passes through the great room several times. On each occasion, the order of the procession is exactly the same; firstly, the White Spear with blood dropping from its tip enters, then two pairs of magnificent candelabra, then the shallow Grail with a single mass wafer upon it and finally a silver tray with a bounty of exotic foods close the procession. When Perceval's cousin inquires of what he saw, she asks first about the bleeding lance, when the Hideous Maiden decries his sins, it is that he didn't ask why the spear bleeds that is her first concern. And lastly, when Perceval swears his oath to the Quest, he states specifically that he must know whom the grail serves and why the spear bleeds.

Obviously, the bleeding lance is as crucial to our under-standing of the nature of the quest, as the grail is. Traditionally, it is believed that the spear was that of Longinus, the centurion who pierced Christ's side, and that the blood is that of the saviour. While this connection may be valid, there is an interpretation of the symbology which makes far more sense, and develops the concept of healing the masculine clearly. The symbol for the lance is also the ancient symbol for that of man, while a symbol of the grail is the corresponding symbol for the woman. The masculine divine is wounded, as demonstrated throughout by Perceval's father, by King Arthur and by the Fisher King and his father.

Between the spear and the grail are a pair of candelabra, candles burning brightly; these traditionally Hebrew symbols for the sacred marriage, indicate the presence of an even more powerful symbol, the Star of David, the union of the spear and grail, the space where spiritual perfection is seen as a by-product of the *hieros gamos*.

One last symbol of the importance of the male/female equilibrium to the Perceval narrative is worth mentioning. The final scene with his hermit/priest/uncle, Perceval is told that the Fisher King's father is sustained by a single mass wafer, given to him daily, by the grail maiden. Though Chretien does at times represent spiritual ideas that might have been questionably heretical at the time, when he does speak specifically of the Christianity it tends to be in a very practically orthodox fashion. Which makes the fact that the old man is in effect receiving communion from a female host, bearing a wholly female symbol, all the more noticeable. This seems a direct attempt by Chretien to put his goddess centred spirituality into Christian terms, a slight reproach against those who do not realise that the host (Jesus Christ) may have the power to sustain, but only through the love of the goddess can joy and happiness be recovered. Thus, Julius Evola might add, 'I wish to emphasize that a very widespread symbolism has seen in the woman a vivifying and transfiguring power, through which it is possible to overcome the human condition.'[30]

There can be no telling if Chretien de Troyes was an orthodox Christian, or if he had been influenced by any of the prevalent goddess cults at the time, but the quest which the poet gives to us, is one that would have taken the honour of women to a sacrilegious level, above that of man. This newfound chivalry, this Love of the Lady, is a Pelagianist quest for redemption; a redemption of Love through the redemption of women. Without the healing, nurturing aspect of female energy, the male energy can only hope to be sustained, but never fully animated, joyful or ecstatic. Each of Perceval's quests is a reflection of his first and most important, a return to the mother, and it is this pursuit for the Great Mother, which he is destined to never fulfil, that allows him to inch closer to moral goodness and spiritual perfection with each new episode.

Chapter 1 References:

1   The quest for the Holy Grail has been recognised in a large number of far more ancient contexts, including the Welsh Mabinogion, the Irish Red Branch cycle and the Saga of Gilgamesh.

2   Some of the grail's various symbolic interpretations include the Cup of the Last Supper, the Philosopher's Stone, a fish platter, a rock and even a chess board.

3   Chretien tells us that he is a vassal of Marie de Champagne and therefore of the Count of Champagne; in addition he is believed to have travelled in England due to his precise descriptions of specific locales.

4   Romanz, meaning simply in the vulgar tongue.

5   (Loomis,1963,p.52)

6   (Barber,2004,pp.10-11)

7   (Jung&vonFranz,1998,p.39)

8   (Jung&vonFranz,1998,p.41)

9   (Chretien,1991,p.387)

10   ibid

11   (Chretien,1991,p.388)

12   (Chretien,1991,pp.388-389)

13   (Chretien,1991,pp.389-390)

14   ibid

15   (Chretien,1991,p.393)

16   (Chretien,1991,p.394)

17   ibid

18   (Chretien, 1991,p.420)

19   ibid

20   (Chretien, 1991,pp.420-421)

21   The sword is commonly understood as a representation of consciousness, the fact that his cousin will tell him that the sword is destined to break, if he uses it in combat, reinforces this.

22   (Chretien, 1991,pp.425-426)

23 (Chretien, 1991,p.438)

24 (Chretien, 1991,p.439)

25 (Chretien, 1991,p.459)

26 ibid

27 ibid

28 (Chretien, 1991,p.460)

29 (Evola, 1997,pp.20-21)

30 (Evola, 1997,p.21)

Bibliography:

Barber, R. 1999, *Myths and Legends of the British Isles*, The Boydell Press.

Barber, R. 2001, *Legends of Arthur*, The Boydell Press.

Barber, R. 2004, *The Holy Grail: Imagination and Belief*, Penguin/Allen Lane.

Bogdanow, F. 'The Mystical Theology of Bernard de Clairvaux,' **in** Noble, P.S. & Paterson, L.M. editors, 1984, *Chretien de Troyes and the Troubadours*, Cambridge, Saint Catherine's College.

Cavendish, R. 1978, *King Arthur and the Grail*, Paladin/Granada Publishing.

Campbell, J. 1968, *The Hero with a Thousand Faces*, 2nd edition, Princeton University Press.

Chretien de Troyes, 1991, 'The Story of the Grail (Perceval)', **in** *Arthurian Romances*, trans. by Kibler, W.W., Penguin Books.

Dunne, J.S. 1973, *Time and Myth*, University of Notre Dame Press.

Evola, J. 1997, *The Mystery of the Grail: Initiation and Magic in the Quest for the Spirit*, trans. by Stucco, G., Rochester, Vermont, Inner Traditions.

Fife, G. 1990, *Arthur the King*, BBC Books.

Graves, R. 1961, *The White Goddess*, Faber and Faber.

Grigsby, J. 2002, *Warriors of the Wasteland*, London, Watkins Publishing.

Jones, P. 'The Grail as Initiation: Jessie Weston and the Vegetation Theory,' **in** Matthews, J. editor, 1990, *The Household of the*

Grail, The Aquarian Press.

Jung, C.G. & Kerenyi, C. 1985, *Science of Mythology*, London, Melbourne and Henley, Ark Paperbacks.

Jung, E. & von Franz, M-L. 1998, *The Grail Legend, Mythos Series*; Princeton University Press.

Kenwrick, J. 1955, *The Religious Quest*, London, SPCK.

Knight, G. *'Dion Fortune and the Grail,'* in Matthews, J. editor, 1990, *The Household of the Grail*, The Aquarian Press.

Kujawski, P. *'In Service of the Psyche,'* in Matthews, J. editor, 1990, *The Household of the Grail*, The Aquarian Press.

Lindsay, J. 1976, *The Troubadours and their World*, London, Frederick Muller Ltd.

Loomis, R.S. 1963, *The Development of Arthurian Romance*, London, Hutchinson University Library.

Matthews, J. 1981, *The Grail: Quest for the Eternal*, Thames and Hudson Press.

Matthews, J. editor, 1984, *At the Table of the Grail: Magic & the Use of Imagination*, London, Boston, Melbourne & Sydney, Routledge & Kegan Paul.

Matthews, J. editor, 1990, *The Household of the Grail*, The Aquarian Press.

Matthews, J. editor, 1996, *Sources of the Grail*, Floris Books.

Noble, P.S. *'Chretien's Arthur,'* in Noble, P.S. & Paterson, L.M. editors, 1984, *Chretien de Troyes and the Troubadours*, Cambridge, Saint Catherine's College.

Noble, P.S. & Paterson, L.M. editors, 1984, *Chretien de Troyes and the Troubadours*, Cambridge, Saint Catherine's College.

Paterson, L.M. 1993, *The World of the Troubadours*, Cambridge University Press.

Paxson, D.L. *'Chretien de Troyes and the Cauldron of Story,'* in Matthews, J. editor, 1990, *The Household of the Grail*, The Aquarian Press.

Pickett, L. 2003, *Mary Magdalene*, London, Robinson.

Shinola Bolen, J. 1994, *Crossing to Avalon*, San Francisco, Harper

Collins.

Waterfield, R. 'Julius Evola: An Italian Interpreter of the Grail,' **in** Matthews, J. editor, 1990, *The Household of the Grail,* The Aquarian Press.

Wolfram von Eschenbach, 1961, *Parzival,* trans. by Mustard, H.M. & Passage, C.E., New York, Vintage Books.

Chapter 2

The Righteous Teachers
By Oddvar Olsen

The Birth of St John the Baptist

The Immaculate Conception mythos is embedded in the human consciousness. This sign of divinity is one of the fundamental beliefs that underpin the Christian faith; however, it was not only Jesus who was born of a virgin. Adonis, Attis, Osiris, Mithra and Dionysus all share the mysterious birth and they all suffered and rose again. Another Immaculate Conception that is often overlooked is the one St Luke describes:

> Luke: 1. 5-7: *"There were in the days of Herod the king of Judea, a certain priest named Zacharias, of the course of Abia: and his wife was of the daughters of Aaron, and her name was Elisabeth. And they were both righteous before God, walking in all the commandments and ordinances of the Lord blameless. And they had no child, because that Elisabeth was barren; and they both were now well stricken in years."*

St Luke, continue in Luke: 1. 11- 13:

> *"And there appeared unto him an angel of the Lord, standing on the right side of the alter of incense. And when Zacharias saw him, he was troubled, and fear fell upon him. But the angel (Gabriel) said unto him. Fear not, Zacharias: for thy prayer is heard; and thy wife Elisabeth shall bear thee a son, and thou shalt call his name John."*

Zacharias doesn't believe a word of what the angel Gabriel tells him and as punishment he is made dumb until the day the miracle unfolds: (Luke: 1. 25) *"And after those days his wife Elisabeth conceived…"* St Luke then continues and tells us about the much more known about Immaculate Conception where the angel Gabriel, six months later visits Jesus' mother Mary; the cousin of Elisabeth: *"And behold thy cousin Elisabeth, she hath also conceived a son in her old age; and this is the sixth month with her who was called barren."* Luke: 1. 36

So here we have another member in the 'Immaculate Conception' club, and, coincidentally, both women from the same family. My initial thought was; " Is St Luke emphasising the importance of Elisabeth's conception by stating that both her and Zacherias: *'both were now well stricken in years'*?" We are not told how old Zacherias is but the implication must be that his age has reduced his ability to father children and that the pregnancy must be God given.

If that was a surprise it was a bigger surprise to understand that Joseph was never mentioned during Gabriel's visit to Mary. Mary is much perplexed when Gabriel approaches her, as we understand of her replies: *"How shall this be, seeing I know not a man?"* (Luke: 1. 34). No man! I thought Mary and Joseph were enjoying a respectable loving marriage. Not so, Mary was single and obviously terribly puzzled. Had I missed something during my misspent religious studies in my student years? I needed to read the other three Gospels as well…

In the hope of finding confirmation of Joseph's and Mary's marriage before consummation I was left blank after reading both *St John* and *St Mark's Gospel,* simply because they don't mention the birth of Jesus! Could *St Matthew's Gospel* advise me in my search? Yes, well no - because Matthew confirms that Mary was single and understandably surprised by Gabriel's claim, as she didn't have a partner. However – Mary conceived accordingly and her son was called Jesus.

Elisabeth's Immaculate Conception is only mentioned in St.

Luke of the four canonical Gospels, and Mary's holy conception in St Matthew and St Luke. The dispute on the historicity of all the Gospels has been raging for years and will most likely continue, together with the debate on the texts found at Nag Hammadi in Upper Egypt in 1945 and the *Dead Sea Scrolls*, found in 1947 and 1956.

Personally, I cannot see any reason why St Luke should mention Elisabeth's Immaculate Conception if it didn't happen. Apart from giving credit to the seraphic potency of Gabriel! When the Bible took shape into the compilation most of us know it today; (and as so many conspiracy theorists suggest there have been many changes agreed by subsequent Diets and convocations) the first thing that the church fathers would have edited out is any possible competition to their favourite 'Son of God', for them to have supplied St John the Baptist with a 'proper' mother. *The Acts of the Apostles* is generally accepted to be a reliable source in the New Testament. Michael Baigent and Richard Leigh confirm this and tell us that the author of 'Acts' identified himself as Luke. They go on to say that Acts could even be the 'second half' of *St Luke's Gospel*. (*The Dead Sea Scrolls Deception*, p. 260) This is suggested because both the *Gospel of St Luke* and *Acts of the Apostles* are addressed to one Theophilus. In the opening of *Acts* the author also refers to his former treatise where he related the story about Jesus' teachings and work. (Acts: 1.1)

What the four Canonical Gospels do agree on is that Jesus travels to the river Jordan, seeking baptism by John. At this time John had become a prevalent prophet and baptiser who often brought together large congregations. When Jesus finds John by Jordan, the four Gospels tells us that many actually believe that John is the long awaited Messiah, the Christ, or even the reincarnated Elias. However, John is humble and as St Mark tells us in Chapter 1. 6 *"And John was clothed with camel's hair, and a girdle of a skin about his loins; and he did eat locust and honey."* The other

Gospels confirm that John is living in remote solitude and preaching in the wilderness. They continue and relate that John denies all claims about his superiority and says that he only baptises with water, but after him one shall come that will *"...baptise you with the Holy Ghost."* Mark: 1. 8.

John's character and popularity would later cause him loose his head at the wish of Herod's enigmatic daughter, Salome. (*Salome*, Yuri Leitch, The Temple # 1)

In 1973, Professor Morton Smith discovered a letter from Clement of Alexandria, which refers to a 'secret apocryphal Gospel of Mark'. Tim Wallace Murphy and Marilyn Hopkins in theirs *Rosslyn – Guardian of the Secrets of the Holy Grail, p. 68*, tells us of this:

> *"Clement's writing discloses a wide-ranging knowledge of early Christian documents, many of which have since been lost or suppressed. Of the Gospel of Mark, Clement was of the opinion that all knowledge of its existence should be denied, in spite of its authenticity, because certain Gnostics had used this document to claim that Jesus had been personally involved in a baptismal cult, in contradiction to Church teachings."*

All the four canonical Gospels agree that Jesus was baptised by St John, and St. Luke suggests that they even were related. Relying on this information it would be of no surprise if Jesus were a part of John's baptismal cult! Christian scholar Professor Morton Smith may as well have denied the existence of the *Gospel of St Luke,* and why not all of them due to their contradictions?

In the non-canonical, *Gospel of Thomas,* which features in the Nag Hammadi codices discovered in 1945, the author tells us:

> *"Among those born of women, from Adam until John the Baptist, there is no one so superior to John the Baptist that his eyes should not be lowered (before him)."*

At first most scholars disregarded the *Gospel of Thomas* and claimed it a second or third century Gnostic forgery, (probably due to its 'non-Christian' content) a fashion adopted by many religious fanatics. However, there is now a growing consensus among scholars that the *Gospel of Thomas*, dates to the very beginnings of the Christian era and may well have taken its first form before any of the four traditional Canonical Gospels.

Familiarities

As I continued reading on these subjects and re-read *The Gospel of Thomas* in more detail, I discovered another interesting statement.

> "*The disciples said to Jesus: We know that you will depart from us. Who is to be our leader? Jesus said to them: Wherever you are, you are to go to James the righteous, for whose sake heaven and earth came into being.*"

In the last chapter we learnt according to St Luke, that John and Jesus were related, they both were also born by mothers unable to bear children (with the aid of the always-resourceful angel Gabriel). When reading the passage above we find another amazing similarity - both designated their leadership to somebody else (within the family) when their death drew close! By John the Baptist advising his followers that the one who baptises with the *Holy Ghost*, was the one to follow after his imminent death i.e. Jesus. And now Jesus refers his disciples to *'James the righteous'*, i.e. *James the Just*, i.e. *Jesus' brother*, who was to continue his ministry!

James the Just, is now accepted by most scholars to be the brother of Jesus and the new leader of Jesus' (and perhaps John the Baptist's and Zacharias) sect in Jerusalem after his crucifixion.

Hugh Schonfield in *The Essene Odyssey* relates another

similarity that suggests that John actually was born in Bethlehem. (p. 49. Hugh is here referring to Mandean texts that were still in existence in Iraq at the time of his writing). Bethlehem is of course where the stories tell us that Jesus was born.

Furthermore, we hardly know anything at all about either John or Jesus, apart from the circumstances of their birth (and that is, in parts, limited) and the few years before they met their death. Why not? We shall try to answer this question momentarily.

If they were 'leaders' of the same 'sect', the most obvious thing to do is to appoint a new leader in time of danger and emergency, and why not to some body they knew well, within their own family?

Another related and important factor is often overlooked. John's father, Zacharias was brutally slain for the sake of his fidelity. During the slaughter of the infants in Bethlehem, he refused to tell Herod's soldiers of the whereabouts of Elisabeth, after she hid in the desert. This unshaken commitment to the safety of his wife and his child cost him his life. This fact is confirmed in the *Gospel Commentaries* of St Ephraim the Syrian (c.373 A.D) and in the *Life of John the Baptist* composed by Serapion c.385-395 A.D. Could this be another similarity? John is perhaps his murdered father's successor, as Jesus was his cousin's (John the Baptist) successor!

The Essenes

The Essene is thought to be the authors of *The Dead Sea Scrolls* found in caves in the vicinity. They were followers of Judaism and started to flourish around the time of the Maccabeean Revolt in 167 B.C - 160 B.C, but were broken up into factions after the Jewish Revolt in 66 A.D. There were various groupings of them, or at least strongly connected to them, such as the Zealots, Nazoreans, Mandaeans and the Ebonites. The Essene leader was called The Righteous Teacher, Zadok or the Lawgiver. This person were not allowed to be called by his name, he was a Priest-King that would be their Messianic liberator and would also lead them through the 'end of times'. A couple of the duties of this leader was to: *"instruct the upright in the knowledge of the Most High"* and to *"teach the wisdom of the Sons of Heaven to the perfect way"* (see Hugh Schonfield, *The Passover Plot*).

After the death of Judas Maccabee, in 160 BC, during the Maccabeean Revolt, many of the Maccabbees had to escape and I believe this was either the start of a strong 'input' to the Essene community at Qumran.

Many have suggested the *Teachers of Righteousness* were of Maccabbeean stock. I asked myself, were there any references to this title going further back. The eminent *Dead Sea Scrolls*, scholar Hugh Schonfield, may provide us with the answer, on p. 5 in *The Essene Odyssey* he tells us:

"The Moreh-Zedek (Teacher of Righteousness comes before us like the mysterious Mechi-zedek (King of Righteousness) in the Epistle to the Hebrews, without father without mother, without ancestry, having neither beginning of days nor end of life (Heb: 8. 3)."

Furthermore, the first century historian Flavius Josephus in his *Antiquities of the Jews* tells us that Jerusalem used to be called Salem and that Melchisedec was *the righteous king* there. After Melchisedec was made *'priest* of God' the name changed to Jerusalem. There are prophesies in Psalms cx. 4: *"Thou art a priest for ever after the order of Mechizedek."* And Hebrews 5:6, 7:17, 21 also predict that the Messiah would be a priest after the Melchisedecian order. Melchisedec is a mysterious character as we not much information is given about him. As we have seen he was a Priest-King and the other thing we know is that he blessed Abraham (Gen: xiv.18).

The Maccabees fulfilled the prophecies and as a new dynasty of Priest-Kings they adopted the title 'Priest of the most high

God' i.e. Melchisedean Priest-King-hood.

The Righteous Teachers

We have now seen that the Maccabees took the title; *'Priest of the most high God'*, this fulfilling the prophesies in Jeremiah, Psalms, Hebrew etc. This was in honour of Melchisedec who was both King and Priest of Righteousness. And in the Essene teachings this person becomes known as 'The Teachers of Righteousness'.

Most scholars have been searching for two Essene leaders, a Royal King and Priest. I think they are wrong and that we are searching for only one person.

Whether Zacharias, the father of John the Baptist was their Teachers of Righteousness I don't know, but perhaps? As he is described in the Bible and earlier scriptures as righteous and he is also a priest. John the Baptist is thought to be the embodiment of Essene teachings by many scholars. As we have seen John is passing on the ministry to Jesus. Jesus was not from Nazareth, but was a Nazorean, his disciple was Simon the Zealot and Jesus often described the *poor* as the chosen ones. The *poor* were a term also used to describe the Ebonites. Of this we may deduct that Jesus had links with the sects mentioned above and therefore a connection to the Essene. Could John the Baptist and Jesus have been doing their training in the Essene community and this is the simple reason why hardly anything is known about the two people that Christianity is built on? As we learnt in the *Gospel of Thomas,* when Jesus were preparing for the long walk up Calvary to Golgotha, he appointed the successor-ship to James the Just i.e. James the Righteous (Teacher).

What they all have in common are being executed under dramatic circumstances. There are clear references for succession in leadership. They are all being described as righteous people and they were all certainly Priests in their own rights.

But none of them became Priest-Kings as Melchisedec was. After the execution of James the Just in 62 A.D. which caused the

Jewish war to break out, the Essene could no more hold their Peace = Zion = Jerusalem = Salem, and they were forced to leave their settlements in Qumran and in and around Jerusalem; a new Exodus began.

The followers of this sect held out for another sixty-five years, until the Second Jewish Revolt of 132 A.D and by that time as the critically acclaimed author Ian Wilson point out in *Jesus the Evidence*, pp 149-150:

> *"...in 62 A.D he (James) was murdered at the instigation of one of the same Sadducee sect responsible for the death of Stephen, and of his brother Jesus. He was subsequently succeeded by Simeon, son of his uncle Cleopas, and by thirteen other Bishops of Jerusalem..."*

Of this statement we can easily reason that a continuation might have occurred through Zacharias, John The Baptist, Jesus and James the Just, Simeon and the other thirteen bishops. And perhaps they even were the *Righteous Teachers* of the Essene community.

The Sons of Brychan
By Yuri Leitch

At the beginning of 2006 I felt a strong desire to visit the wondrous waterfall of St. Nectan's Glen, near Tintagel. A heart pulling desire that persisted into the spring. By happy circumstances I was given the opportunity to stay at the Camelot Castle hotel, Tintagel, for free! So I found myself at this beautiful sacred site (of suspected Druidic initiations) during bluebell abundant May.

Little did I realise until I got there that my visit would have continuing repercussions upon some of my fields of research. One of which, I thought I had drawn to a conclusion (see my article 'Sinclair, the mystery of the name' in issue 8 of *The Temple*; - where I discussed the most likely origin of the name 'Sinclair' to a 6th century Cornish saint (St. Cleer) and told of his tragic death, being decapitated by two knights, and how, miraculously, the headless body of St. Cleer carried his own head to a sacred well, before dying.)

Imagine my surprise then, when I learnt that St. Nectan was St. Cleer's older brother! Both sons of the famous King Brychan of Wales. Stranger still is that both brothers died in almost identical ways. St. Cleer was beheaded by two knights and St. Nectan was beheaded by two robbers. Both brothers pick up their decapitated heads and each carries it to a sacred well. One wonders if this fate wasn't some odd family tradition or curse? It's one thing to create a Holy Well, but losing your head to do so, seems a tad extreme! Maybe the family had enemies?

Cornwall has long been known as the 'land of the saints' and has numerous place names remembering these saints. St Ives, St Austell, St Agnes (just a few off the top of my head) even places that are not prefixed by 'St' are named after saints, like

Perranporth (St. Pirran) and Mevagissey, derived from 'Saint Meva 'and' (in Cornish 'hag') saint Issey'.

These Cornish saints date back to the 5th, 6th and 7th centuries, Britain's so called 'Dark Ages' and are the shadows of the old 'Celtic Church' (all but erased by Catholicism and the Church of England.)

Many of these saints came to Cornwall (or Kernow, as it was once called) from the great schools and monastic libraries of Ireland and from the landmass we now call Wales. ('Wales' is an insult name of spite, derived from the Saxon word 'Waellas', which means 'Foreigners'. So too is Cornwall, once 'Kernow' but now derived from the Saxon 'Cern-Waellas' ('the foreigners of Kernow')

One group of Cornwall's saints, were all of one family, siblings, men and women, often numbering twenty-four individuals (though the counting can fluctuate depending upon the sources). This family is known as the 'Children of Brychan'. (I have titled this essay 'The Sons of Brychan' because I am focusing specifically upon two of the brothers, but there are many sisters too, so 'Children of' is a more correct title.)

This family of saints was the offspring of the 'Welsh' King Brychan, whose small kingdom was known of as 'Brycheiniog', today known as the Brecon Beacons. Brychan and his offspring were of ancient Irish descent (evidence is apparent by the many Ogham inscribed stones found upon their territories.) 'Brycheiniog' means 'of the Speckled Tartan'.

The 'Welsh Triads' record the importance of Brychan's children. Triad 81 says,

'The Three Saintly lineages of the Island of Britain; - The lineage of Joseph of Armathea; and the lineage of Cunedda Wledigi; and the lineage of Brychan Brycheiniog.

Another version says,

'Three kindreds of saints of the Island of Britain, by a Welsh mother; - The offspring of Brychan Brycheiniog; and the offspring of Cunedda Wledig; and the offspring of Caw of Pictlan).

We also learn from the Welsh Triads (96; 'Three Wives whom Brychan Brycheiniog had'). That the twenty-four 'Children of Brychan' stemmed from three mothers (three Queens; - three crowns) whose names are given as Eurbrawst, Rybrawst, and Peresgri.

The Children of Brychan have places named after them, throughout Cornwall, Devon, Brittany and Normandy. Their legends are too numerous for me to give justice to here, but of interest to scholars of Arthurian studies, this family of saints has many connections to the stories of King Arthur. Brychan himself was a staunch ally of Vortigern and gave him shelter against Ambrosius (characters from Merlin's story) The main church upon the cliffs at Tintagel is that of St Madron (who was Vortigern's grandaughter) and Brychan's daughter St Juliot, founded the 6th century monastery upon the headland at Tintagel (Arthur's legendary birthplace; and underneath the headland is 'Merlin's Cave') Another of Brychan's daughters is St. Endellion, she is King Arthur's god daughter. Through the Children of Brychan, Tintagel had Arthurian connections long before the medieval Arthurian Romances and Tennyson.

The map on the next page depicts locations around the vicinity of Bodmin Moor, which are named after some of the Children of Brychan. For me it is a fascinating area of Cornwall. In Bodmin Moor is the tiny village of Temple, with its church situated upon old Templar lands. And the great 'Michael Line' alignment cuts through the lower area of the moor, passing through the 'Hurlers' stone circles. The Michael Line is fixed upon the Beltaine (May 1st) sunrise and St. Teath (another of Brychan's daughters) to the north west of Bodmin Moor, has her feast day on the 1st of May!

At the north of Bodmin Moor is St. Clether and to the south is St. Cleer (Clether and Cleer are the same person, the namesake of Saint Clair-sur-Epte in Normandy, from whence the Sinclairs take their name.)

In this one area you have Templar associations; Sinclair intrigue; Tintagel and all its related Arthurian traditions and the 'Saintly lineage' of Brychan Brecheiniog (Who in the Welsh Triads is counted along with the descendants of Joseph of Arimathea, as one of the three saintly lineages). The contents of this map create a grail seekers hotbed!

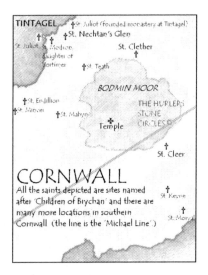

Of all of Cornwall, the Knights Templar chose this area to be their Cornish headquarters!

As with all histories of Britain's 'Dark Ages' there is little in the way of contemporary evidence and the lives of these saints have taken on mythic qualities; - like King Arthur, and like Saint Bridget of Kildare, who appears to of been a real living person and yet also possibly, the christianised version of the native British goddess Bride (or the saint was named after the goddess, and embodied her in some way?) The Children of Brychan seem to be more than human.

There are many different (medieval and later) sources about this family of saints. One source counts them as numbering 12, another says 36, and another says 24 daughters and 24 brothers; but the most constant counting is 24; - of course, all these numbers are multiples of 12 and if each were a month, some researchers have suggested, then they are probably some kind of lost zodiacal/year deities, turned into saints. I'm not convinced about this '12 month' theory and doing things in twelves is quite a Celtic Church tradition; - St. Columba founded Iona along with 12 companions and according to legend, Joseph of Arimathea went to Glastonbury with 12 companions.

Saint Nectan was the eldest of the children and was the first to leave his father's home. He crossed the Sabrina Sea (Bristol Channel) to north Devon and lived as a hermit at a place, now called Stoke, near Hartland Point. This is where his Holy Well is located and the local church is dedicated to him (it has a nice stained glass window of King Arthur and the Holy Grail.) All of Nectan's brothers and sisters followed in his example and they all lived in Devon and Cornwall as hermits. Once a year they would all go to Hartland Point, on New Years Eve, a family gathering at the eldest brother's home and then they would return back to their hermetic lives.

In May this year when I visited Saint Nectan's Glen, I sat for over an hour and drew the waterfall.

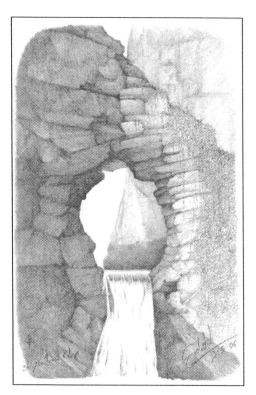

As I drew, I had some ideas about Saint Nectan and my ideas surprised me. It's overall ambiance and feeling is very old, pagan, feminine and Faerie. It was hard to feel the presence of a male Christian hermit.

Saint Nectan like Saint Bridget, could also be an ancient British deity, or in some way, embody that deity. 'Nectan' is the Cornish variant of his name. In Latin he is 'Nathanus' ('Nathan' in modern English) but in Welsh he is 'Nudd' (which is pronounced 'Neath') One of my other fields of research at the moment is a study of Gwyn ap Nudd, the ancient god of Glastonbury Tor ('ap' just means 'son of' and so Nudd is Gwyn's father. Gwyn is the lord of the British 'other-(faerie)-world'.) According to legend, the last resting place of the Faerie is the 'Vale of Neath' in the south of Wales. 'St. Nectan's Glen' and the 'Vale of Neath' are place names that mean exactly the same thing. They are identical descriptions, meaning 'Nudd's Vale/Glen'.

Nudd is the great River God of Britain, he represents the Milky Way, the river of the heavens. He is a god of primordial chaos and also of healing. There is a Romano British temple of his near the River Severn at Lydney, where he is remembered as 'Nodens'. The River Severn is Britain's most powerful (tidal extreme) river. Saint Nectan's Glen is an awesome natural waterfall, that comes crashing down into a bowl of natural rocks and then gushes forth through a hole in those rocks to become a stream that winds its way down to the coast near Tintagel, through the beautiful faerie-like, Rocky Valley. The source of rivers as a life-giving/healing thing. Is it any wonder that both St Cleer and St Nectan with the last ounce of their life-force, take their heads to Sacred Wells which are then venerated and used for healing by local people for many centuries after?

Still today, at St. Nectan's Holy well, I found the remains of candle wax and a few ribbons tied to the overhanging branches, that surround the well; and wondrous Saint Nectan's Glen is adorned by masses of ribbons, stones (with peoples names scratched upon them), photos of loved ones, coins crammed into little crevices. Wonderful, that in the 21st century, the waters of life are still treasured and valued, and that a few places are still held sacred.

Sinclair - The Mystery of the Name
By Yuri Leitch

Who were the Sinclairs? The now legendary surname, popularized by 'The Holy Blood and the Holy Grail,' promoted as an ancient Grail lineage by the *Preure de Sion,* and the creative genius of that most enigmatic building, Roslyn Chapel.

They first arrive on the historical stage as supportive companions to William the Conqueror in 1066, part of the Norman elite. They came from the Normandy town of 'St. Clair' and it is from their town of origin that it is believed that they are named... but herein lays a mystery.

The namesake of the Sinclair's hometown, Saint Clare, according to the Oxford dictionary of Saints, lived between 1194 and 1253 (and she wasn't 'sainted' until 1257). The problem is this; - Richard de St. Clair was in the saddle, alongside William the Conqueror in 1066, a hundred and ninety years before Clare became a saint! One hundred and twenty eight years before she was even born.

So, however the Sinclair's hometown got its name, it was nothing to do with miss Saint Clare.

The Conqueror's friend, Richard de St. Clair had his surname spelt in many different variations. Wace records him as 'St. Cler', the *Domesday Book* (which was partly compiled by Adam St. Clair) records Richard as 'de Sencler', and the Register of the Monks of Castleacre call him 'Sancto Cleer'... So what is to be made from all of this?

I knew of a 'St. Cleer' from previous areas of research. I pondered whether this could be the explanations to 'St Cler', 'de Sencler' and 'Sancto Cleer'... but at first appearance this didn't seem to make any sense at all as St. Cleer was a 6th century Welsh hermit who settled in Cornwall. What possible connection could there be between a Welsh hermit and the aristocratic elite of Norman England? I thought that the Sinclairs were of Norman (some (*the Priure de Sion*) say Merovignion) origins... I had to look into this and figure out who were the Normans.

The Normans are from an area of France called Normandy. In the year 911 King Charles 'the Simple' of France, after being troubled by a Viking warlord called Rollo, gave Rollo northern France in a desperate bid for peace... this part of northern France then became known as 'Normandy'. Rollo the warlord became a duke and married a French princess.

It really is a cultural error to see the Normans as 'Men of the North' in a 'Norse' or Viking type perspective. For sure, along with Rollo came many Vikings but the French of northern France remained where they were and absorbed Rollo and his kin, as he absorbed Normandy by becoming a duke and marrying into French aristocracy.

The Normans who invaded England in 1066 were mostly French speaking noblemen of northern France, not Norse speaking Vikings.

Normandy is about the size of Cornwall and Devon combined, and as the crow flies, is closer to London than Yorkshire. If you take a boat across the English Channel you'll land in Normandy, a journey that many Britons had made for centuries. West of Normandy and directly below Devon and Cornwall is Brittany. Brittany and Normandy both have many place-names named after Welsh and Cornish saints, in fact, by the time of William's conquering there had been over a thousand years of interaction back and forth across the channel between Cornwall, Devon, Dorset and Brittany and Normandy. This collection of peoples shared the same 'Celtic' origins.

This common ancestry (that wasn't shared by the Saxons of England (who came from what is now Germany and Denmark) probably explains why the Normans made a triumphant hero out of King Arthur (a Briton) and the Saxons throughout their 500 years of rule, never did; the Saxons after all, were Arthur's old enemy. As for the Normans being 'Norse', why should the 'Norse-men' make a hero out of a Dark Age Welsh king? The Normans were only 'men of the north' to the southern French; in my opinion, only a few of them were of Viking descent;- what few descendants there were of Duke Rollo's men, the rest of William's 'nobles' were of old British and Breton aristocracy.

So, although not provable, a Welsh/Breton origin for the Sinclair family is certainly very, very possible. So who was this Welsh hermit, St. Cleer?

It was at the end of King Arthur's time, the so called 'Dark Ages', around the 6th century, that as more and more Saxons invaded and England began to swell, what was left of the 'Romano-British' natives began to move in large numbers away from England. Those of the Wiltshire, Dorset and Somerset areas moved away and settled in Wales, Devon and Cornwall (even to the north of France) This influx caused a domino effect of more movement within the refuge realms of Wales and Cornwall. It is from this era that we have the tales of the 'Children of Brychan'.

Brychan was a Welsh King of the late 5th century, of the Breacon Beacons area of southern Wales. He had twenty-four children (boys and girls). The legends of the Children of Brychan are vast and numerous but in brief, each one of them moved across the Bristol Channel to Cornwall and Devon, and each lived as hermit and spread the word of Celtic Christianity wherever they went. All of them have places in Devon, Cornwall, Brittany and Normandy named after them. All 24 children became saints. St. Cleer was one of the sons of Brychan (Cleer was also known as 'Clether' and 'Clarus') he gives his name to St. Clither a small village on the northern edge of Bodmin Moor, Cornwall (close to the village of Alternun, named after another 5th century saint, 'Nonna', she went on to Brittany where her tomb still stands) He also gives his name to the small village on the southern edge of Bodmin Moor, still called till this very day, St. Cleer (close by to the village of St. Keyne (Cleer's sister)). There is also a place named St. Claro in Brittany; it isn't difficult to imagine this Welsh hermit being the namesake of the town from whence sprung the Sinclair family.

(The alternative to this theory is that Richard de Sencler (1066) was named after an Italian saint who was still 128 years away from being born)!

More 'Light' is shed upon this enigma when we look into the meaning of the name. In Welsh, 'claer' means 'clear, shining, bright' and 'cler' means 'Bards, Minstrels' and 'clera' means 'travelling Bards, Minstrels'.

All this is pregnant with suggestions worthy of much serious contemplation. The stories of the Grail (of which the *'Preure de Sion'* believed the Sinclairs to be guardians of) are the early stories put into literature, stories originally told by travelling Bards and Troubadours. Here we have the likely origin of the Sinclair name 'cler, claer, clera' having the likely meaning of 'travelling story tellers of the 'Light' (just like Brychan's 24 children spreading their 'light' of Celtic Christianity). In the Welsh Triad (81) it says; *'The Three saintly lineages of the Island of Britain; The lineage of Joseph of Arimathea; and the lineage of Cunedda Wledig; and the lineage of Brychan Brycheiniog')* From these three families came most of the saints of the *'Celtic Church'*. This hints at a possible (if only intellectual) connection between the Sinclair bloodline and that of Joseph of Arimathea!

Maybe the Sinclairs did know something very special, a tradition of 'knowledge' past down from generation to generation; and then travelled around telling their 'story'.

When the Saxons first invaded they were pagan souls but in time they adopted the Christianity of the Roman Catholic Church. The problem with this is that Britain already had its own 'Celtic Church' (which in many ways was a very different doctrine to that of Rome). In the year 664 the 'Synod of Whitby' (of Saxon England) abolished the 'Celtic Church'. The Christianity of King Arthur and Joseph of Arimathea and of all the Children of Brychan became heresy. To the Saxon monarchs Arthur was a heretical king not a hero. It would be left to the so-called 'Normans' of the 11th century to make a hero out of a heretical Celtic Christian king, and within that literary construct hide their 'light' and knowledge of the Grail, of Joseph of Arimathea and of a very alternative understanding to the life and times of Jesus than was told by Catholic dogma. In an era when death was the common punishment for heretical beliefs; story- books can't be heretical can they? Surely they're just simple stories, fireside entertainment... no?

New Relevations

I had thought that at this stage of writing that I had reached completion of this article. I emailed some copies to friends to read. My friend, the historical author Andrew Collins, was kind enough to point out some (what at first appeared) conflicting information that was to shed a lot more light on this subject. He told me about an event called the 'Treatise of St. Clair-sur-Epte', which took place in the year 911, thus predating Richard de St. Clair's presence during the Norman Conquest, and that this event embodied yet a different Saint Clair.

At first I felt a little jaded that I had written all the above in vain but happily that is not how things have turned out.

The fascinating thing about the 'Treatise of St. Clair-sur-Epte' is that it takes us back to the origin of Normandy. This treaty was the agreement signed by Rollo the Viking warlord and King Charles 'the simple' of France; signed by both of them when Charles gave Rollo 'Normandy' in his desperate bid for peace. Looking on the Internet I found a fascinating web page (among many)... http://sinclair.quarterman.org/who/hermit/20020626.html

... This page gives a detailed explanation of what appears to be another St. Clair. The source of this St. Clair story is given as one Mr Philippe Sinclair (no archive literary source is given).

According to Mr Philippe Sinclair this other historical Saint Clair was a man, born in Rochester, Kent, England around 845 A.D. Born of wealthy parents. He became a Christian hermit and travelled around France, finally settling down at a holy well around which grew the town of 'St. Clair-sur-Epte', about 15 miles southwest of Gisors.

The legend told by Philippe Sinclair is (in short) thus; An English noble woman had been spurned by St. Clair because he had refused to marry her! She sent two knights to find him and kill him (women spurned eh?) In time, the two knights arrive at the holy well where St. Clair had made his home. They ask him, 'Do you know a man named St. Clair'? The hermit says that he doesn't know anyone of that name, then, riddled with Christian guilt he confesses that he is the St. Clair that they are looking for.

One knight then draws his sword and cuts off St. Clair's head!

After he is decapitated the headless saint picks up his head and dips it into the holy well, then he carries it off to the church of St Clair-sur-Epte, before finally lying down and dying. The two knights left his body where it was but took his head back to England, their ship sank on their way home and St. Clair's head was lost.

Although this legend is fascinating (as anything with decapitated heads stinks of Grail and Templarisms) this legend seemed to me to be a very garbled story. For a start, the Oxford Dictionary of Saints (a pretty good source book) does not acknowledge the existence of any 9th century St. Clair from Rochester and looking around the Internet I haven't been able to find any confirmation that there ever was a St. Clair from Rochester.

What is interesting though is that the two knights should want to know whether he was 'St. Clair' and that he should first deny his 'name' then confess, ensuring his imminent execution. I suspected that all this was a garbled memory of the original Welsh saint who like the Rochester saint of the same name was also a male hermit. Further more, the date given by Philippe Sinclair for the beheading of St. Clair was the 4th November 884 A.D. This confirms my suspicions, as the 4th of November is also the feast day of St. Cleer of Cornwall. Surely these two male hermits, called 'Clair', both remembered on the 4th November are one and the same person?

I would assume that at St. Clair-sur-Epte we have the final resting place of the Welsh hermit, the travelling 'Bard of enlightenment', St. Cleer and that the 9th century legends are a garbled memory of his final resting place.

It is fascinating then, to have a possible direct connection between the 6th century St. Cleer and Richard de St. Clair at the Battle of Hastings;

That this final resting place was chosen as the location above all others for the treatise and 'birth' of Normandy; is also fascinating food for thought. Why here at this humble town came the King of France and not to Gisor, which was only 15 miles away?

The King Arthur Code
Philip Gardiner

The answer to the question, *"what is the Holy Grail?"* is a complex one, as I myself was to discover. There are many prejudices surrounding the origin and I am uniquely situated to see these prejudices as a marketing man. These prejudices are the very things we in the marketing world attempt to change or more properly, use.

If it were not difficult enough trying to sift through hundreds of texts on the Grail, it was now made harder by the propaganda story makers of ages past. But in the end all of these pre-conceived problems are irrelevant.

Evidence for where the idea of the Grail originated is widespread, difficult and practically impossible, and it is my opinion that it must come from several sources, all of which, if I am right, did actually originate from the same generic source, if not the same place. We must therefore look for our goal in history, ancient texts, etymology, religion and strangely science. With all this in mind I found every book, text and viewpoint I could and spent hour after hour deep in the mystery of the Grail.

The difficulties I found were eventually straightforward. Who could claim the origin of the Grail? And would this itself give me evidence for the theory I was now part of.

The Grail is now fundamentally a European idea. This was not always the case. Although, many scholars point to Celtic origins, an equal amount disagree, pointing to a purely romantic, almost modern Christian origin.

The Celtic and Christian legends I soon discovered, as many have before me, were simple adaptations and overlaying of new ideas onto old truths. All this, serving to hide the real facts even deeper from us, whether by design or accident. We must also overcome the Gnostic ideology, which points towards the esoteric and enlightenment aspects of the Grail myths. In the end, whichever idea we attach ourselves onto, they all point to one unique and simple conclusion - we can obtain eternal life through the Grail.

I believe that there is also a literal truth to the Grail myth. My belief is that quite simply over vast periods of time the symbolism surrounding the Grail has only served to hide the truth of it's origins. That the origins of the Grail were lost, or hidden, and the real, literal truth forgotten. Instead, the words and symbols took on the magical element themselves and the power of the original and magical Grail device became mere words. When the truth is lost, the legend lives on, and the power of the legend can grow. The same thing happens today and if this happens to us now, in our over populated information age, then it certainly happened in the past. We need only look at Robin Hood and King Arthur for confirmation of the fact that somewhere we lost the truth and the propaganda men took over.

And one of those characters is intrinsically linked with our story here. Attached most strongly to the Grail lore is the legendary story of King Arthur. This attachment gives us our best clue as to the origins of the Grail. The Arthur tales are now very well known and have been extensively researched and commented upon by thousands of other authors. However, most people are totally unaware, as was I, that even now the meaning and origin of this tale is hotly debated. It is seeming more and more likely that the influence of the surrounding and distance cultures were swallowed up into the various elements of the Arthur cycle and therefore no one specific origin of the story can be directly pinpointed - the Arthur myth is an accumulation of many sources. However, what we will discover is that all these influences point back themselves to the same source for the Grail myth. No matter where the various original sources came from, they all had the same origin in one great secret, and I believed that I knew what it was. Not only that, it seemed more and more obvious that I was alone in this discovery.

Now I decided that the elements, which concern the Grail myth, should be looked at closely if I were to reveal the next stage of the Grail journey.

Arthur's Clues

In the claimed Celtic origins for the Arthur legends, we are told that the Grail is a cauldron, a fertility and immortality symbol - the basic, but most powerful, religious icon of it's day. It issued forth marvellous and magical feasts, revitalising and resurrecting great and powerful armies. Let's have a look at some examples of this particular element of ancient myth.

In Celtic mythology we find the 'Cauldron of the Head of Hades', which was to be found at Caer Pedryvan, the 'four cornered castle' or 'fire castle'. This was a special and magical place, where the people were said to drink sparkling wine. There are here a few clues for our journey, some magical pointers or codes to guide us in the right direction.

Firstly, the cauldron is of the Head of Hades, the god of the afterlife. Why the head? There is throughout mythology and folklore, and indeed, history, a strong tradition surrounding the symbolism of heads and head worship. This I knew from my previous research.

We find people keeping the heads of the vanquished as a great prize and it was even said that it would give extended life! A new twist. It was regarded as one of the chief members of the body. It was the seat of life force, carrying the soul. There is even a tale told that Arthur dug up the head of Bran the Blessed, which had been buried to protect England. This head was known as Uther Ben or 'wonderful head'.

Now, as I have said this Cauldron of the Head of Hades, was said to be found at Caer Pedryvan and Pedraven strangely means newt. In Cornish a newt or more properly in etymology 'an ewte' (which means resplendent mind and the tails of newts were illustrated as the Hebrew symbol Yod, the symbol for Jehovah), was a lizard, serpent or dragon. It also features on the breast of the wise Minerva - the snake goddess of Rome - wisdom being one of the attributes of the serpent. As I pointed out the word for a newt was Pedraven. Pear means four or fire or father. So Pendryvan (sounding remarkably like Pendragon) could mean father of Evan, the Welsh Bacchus or Dionysus. Bacchus was the serpent god of wine and the people at Caer Pedryvan drank sparkling wine, so this link could well have some foundation. The magical cauldron was therefore kept at the place of Evan/Bacchus, the serpent's head! I had to question this idea. Why would the Grail be kept at the place of the serpent's head? Two elements which appeared to me again and again - the head and the serpent. Both of these were becoming more and more important.

Thirdly, Caer Pedryvan was also called Caer Sidi, which was another name for Stonehenge. Diodorus Siculus called Stonehenge the Temple of Apollo. What possible connections with my theory could be found in this strange association with Stonehenge? I decided to look at Apollo and was amazed yet again to find that Apollo was the god of healing and wielded the now famous caduceus, a staff entwined about by two serpents. The caduceus is said to have been created when Hermes struck two warring snakes apart with a staff and is now the symbol of healing and has always been a symbol for immortality. Are we seeing any links here yet?

Well, Caer Sidi has been related to a spinning wheel in etymological circles, with arrows of poison shooting from many holes. It was called the Omphallus, suggesting Om Phallus, the ever enkindling (immortal) light, Zodiac, Axis or Elixir, and the spores of the mighty Hueel (Hu = light, eel = snake) (See, *The Lost Language of Symbolism,* Harold Bayley). So Stonehenge, the Temple of Apollo in myth, is not only linked with serpents via mythology, but also linked with the poison and the Elixir.

The link so far, in case you have not guessed is the snake.

The origins of these wonderful tales - mainly Celtic and Greek mythology - also tell us that the snake was deeply associated with healing and water. For instance, Sirona, the Gaulish goddess, was a healing goddess, with snakes entwined about her arm. Sirona means star, and she had healing shrines associated with Grannos, which amazingly is yet another name for Apollo. She was also associated with regeneration and resurrection - immortality.

Ireland was said to have been a huge centre for healing, and again we find similar healing and snake related gods. Dian Cecht, who killed Meich (Meich was the son of Morrigan and was said to have had three hearts, each one containing a serpent). This deity was god of healing and was fabled to have dipped the mythical Tuatha De Danaan into a cauldron of regeneration to save them. Three sons brought three healers, the holy trinity from the snake goddess, symbolised by the cauldron.

This is all surely revealing something to us. That the ancient Celtic peoples venerated the healing power of the snake and often symbolised it with a cauldron or alternatively that the cauldron was a vessel for the healing snake. Plutarch said, "The men of old time associated the serpent most of all beasts with heroes" and indeed it does seem that all heroes in one form or another have serpents among their symbols.

All of this is just a small hint at the evidence, which is yet to come on our journey. But the Arthur legend holds many more clues to the origin of the Grail. I was quickly discovering that there are hints almost everywhere.

Arthur was the son of Uther Pendragon. Uther (which means wonderful), like Aither, the father of Pan, may be equated in etymology to Ether, the superfine, all permeating atmosphere otherwise known as Zeus. So Uther or Zeus was the father of Arthur, Arthur was therefore the Son of God, like Jesus. Arthur was said to have had a stronghold at Tintagel, which was alternatively known as Dundagel - dun d ag el actually means The Stronghold of the Resplendent Mighty God.[1]

The title, Pendragon, was understood as the King of Kings, not just by the Britons, but also by the Chinese Manchu and the Phoenicians. Pen, meaning head, making Pendragon, literally the 'head of the dragon.' Now, dragon, obviously, in mythological terms is the same as the serpent and snake. The dragon eventually is the standard of the West Saxons, the Welsh, the Phoenicians and the Chinese Manchu dynasty, among others. Another point to note and remember, that the dragon was seen as red, on a white background. These colours will become very important later on in our investigation and we will find in the Arthur tales the battles betweens white and red dragons. However, most intriguing is the use of the head again in the very name of the key player, it of course being linked together with the dragon/serpent.

There is another thread to follow here as well. The link with Uther to Zeus brings us to the ideas put forward by Howard Reid in his fascinating book 'Arthur - the Dragon King'. Howard Reid claims that much of the Arthur cycle can be traced to the Scythians.

The Scythians were brought to Britain from the Steppes by the Romans as a mercenary horseback fighting force. This employing of mercenaries was a not an uncommon practice in antiquity. Many alliances between various groups were formed and then broken. And all along, as these warriors were thrashing out the great political power battles of the day, subtle transferences of folklore, traditions and legends were passed about, not to mention religion. These myths were spread with the wars and movements of armies and it is in this way that the Scythians brought their beliefs with them to Britain.

One remarkable similarity is the peculiar rituals of the sword, in which there is a ritual of thrusting the blood soaked blade into the ground and drawing it out slowly. An insightful Arthurian link with the drawing of the sword from the stone or anvil.

However, my first link was that of Uther to Zeus. This Zeus god of the Scythians and Greeks is said to have visited Olympias in the form of a serpent and between them they procreated a special line of humans which eventually led to Alexander the Great - a kind of serpent bloodline. This tale is too similar to the Arthurian legend to be coincidence as Uther is said to have shape shifted himself in-order to visit Igranie, the wife of the Duke of Tintagel, who gave birth to Arthur, another great warrior leader like Alexander. We must note that the original story did involve the hero becoming the snake in-order to create the life of a powerful and vibrant warrior. And it is a bloodline of the snake worshippers, which also protects the Grail.

These Scythians also had a practice of attaching the severed heads of their defeated to the saddle, as if to scare off any future combatant. All the heads of the warriors killed in the battle were taken to the King, who would pay a dividend of the booty. More startlingly in relation to the Holy Grail is the fact that they would also cut off the top of the skull, clean it out, gild it and turn this macabre sight into a mystical drinking vessel. So, for some reason, we have the people who worship the snake shape shifting Zeus, revering heads and drinking blood - the life essence. This practice however was extremely widespread and by no means reserved just for this warrior group. Golden heads have been found far and wide, and it was not always enemy heads, which were used. Nobody is sure where this practice originated. But it did originate in an area, which has profound links with serpent worship. I also found evidence that Tantric Skull cups had been used for mixing a "divine substance of the snake."

The appearance of an actual cup or chalice is, as we have seen, a late addition to the Arthurian canon, although we have now seen that it was just a Christianised addition of an earlier Celtic and Scythian tradition. The cup took on the mystical element of the head and is the very symbol of regeneration, resurrection and immortality. These cups, chalices and cauldrons all become grouped together in the legends and roughly speaking, we find ourselves searching for them in sacred sites. In Arthur's stories we are sent upon a special quest, to search out a maiden, or save a land from devastation, or indeed discover the Holy Grail. Here we shall find a maiden or holy lady. She is always a semi-divine being, almost a deity or spirit. Her colour is always white. These women in Celtic or other ancient pagan legends are always associated with snakes or serpents. In fact in one story this is quite blatant as one particular snake is transformed into a beautiful maiden. Arthur's wife, Guinevere is likened to a crowned serpent, a Royal Snake, by the symbol of the Royal Sarassins, an ancient legendary and serpentine race of Britain.

The maiden is seen either as a prisoner in some great tower or enchantress like Eve with the apple. Either way, she draws in the knight-errant to her cause. With this maiden we find a champion protector, usually in the form of a black knight. The newcomer must be victorious in his battle with the black knight in-order to gain his prize, which is often seen as being a night spent with the magical snake maiden.

The important part of this however is the blood of the vanquished. The black knights blood is said to have the power to heal and bestow eternal life and indeed yet again it is the head of the knight from which spews the most powerful blood.

King Arthur himself in *Perlesvaus* is sent off on a voyage by Guinevere the snake queen. Eventually, after coming to a magical clearing he finds a maiden seated at the foot of a tree. She shows Arthur to the chapel, which he seeks, where a black knight appears and hurls a lance of fire into Arthur's arm. Fortunately the blood of Pendragon extinguishes the flames and Arthur goes on to kill the knight. Twenty other knights then appear and finish the job, by hacking the corpse to pieces. Arthur takes the head to the maiden who anoints his arm with the blood of the head and he is miraculously healed. The maiden then tells how she can now use to the head restore her fortunes.

The *red* dragon of Arthur Pendragon, the serpent King, is sent off by the *white* serpent queen to rescue one of their kind and restore her fortune. The dark knight is a simple replacement of the dragon guardian of thousands of other popular worldwide myths. The maiden is seated at the foot of the tree of life and knowledge, as she herself is a symbol of wisdom. The lance launched by the black knight is the serpents/dragons fiery poison. Only by taking the blood of the serpent can Arthur achieve the antidote and this is what happens as Arthur's blood extinguishes the flames of pain. The head of the serpent has both the poisonous glands of the serpent and the healing blood, the red and the white. The blood from this head therefore becomes the all-healer, the life eternal and resurrecting power. Could we have here the secret of the head and serpent myths? Could there be a literal truth hidden behind these medieval myths? Suddenly it was becoming clear that the head of the serpent was the most important element to these ancient storytellers.

It is now well known that people such as the knight's Templar were said to have worshipped severed heads in one form or another.

The knights Templar are a fascinating historical group. Warrior monks destined for greatness, and yet also destined for a great fall. They are claimed to have been an order of Christian knights of the 12th to 14th centuries, and yet much of their tradition and writings show a clear Gnostic belief, which is, at this time more attuned to the Mandean thoughts, not Christian ideas. Mandeans or Disciples of John still exist to this day in Syria and Palestine, sometimes under the title of Druzes. In Basra, Persia, they take the name Mandean still. All these groups have one common origin - the so-called heresies of the Nazareans (Nasoreans) or Ophites (serpent worshippers). The Ophitic snake symbolism goes back right through Greek,

Egyptian and Phrygian cultures, encompassing such ideas as conquest over death, immortality and wisdom and opens out into a group of ancient snake cults such as Ophite-Cainites, Ophite-Sethian and Ophite-Nachaites - all evolving eventually into the Gnostic tradition of the Ouroboros, a universally emerging symbol of the ancient beliefs, a symbol for immortality.

Mandeans have no belief in Jesus as the only Son of God, or his so-called scriptures, placing instead their faith in St John and Sophia - wisdom. As you will know, John lost his head, which was offered up on the sacred plate to Salome as being the greatest prize and the platter is often said to be a symbol of the Grail itself. John was an Ophite; a member of those who worship the snake and the term Sophia (S'Ophia) comes from this very cult. Snakes have in fact been symbolic of Sophia or Wisdom ever since ancient times. In etymology, ophts is Latin for serpent or stone (lithos), so we have the serpent also as a stone, which must remind us of Wolfram von Eschenbach's notion of the Grail as a stone, a double ploy in language, created to hide the snake and pointing to the link between the Grail and the Philosophers Stone. Nazareans (Nasurai) were also worshippers of snakes. The faith therefore was in the serpent's head for immortality. The fact remains that the Gnostic symbol of wisdom and immortality, the symbol of the saviour is the snake entwined about the tau cross or Sacramental loaf. The bread of life was the serpent.

Another, historical, point to note here is that of Ambrosia. Ambrosia means literally food or nectar of the gods or Elixir. It is said that a certain Ambrosius Aurelianus, a 5th century figure mentioned by Gildas as being the last of the Roman nation in Britain, under whose leadership they rallied to resist the Saxons, may have been Arthur's father, uncle or indeed Arthur himself. Ambrosius was a great leader and a modest man, according to Gildas, whose parents were undoubtedly of the purple. Ambrosius died in approximately 495ad so the dates are about right for him to have been Arthur's father or uncle.

There probably was an Ambrosius, Arthur and Vortigern. They probably fought great battles and overcame terrible troubles, but would they understand our idea of the Grail today? I doubt it. What they would understand however, would be a magical substance which could help soldiers recover, heal wounds, almost resurrect them in great numbers. This substance was mixed in the Holy Mixing Bowl (kpa=mixing bowl and is the origin of cup). And this is why, as many scholars have pointed out, there are many Holy Grails. There are many mixing bowls, but all share the one secret.

I will end with an exert from Wolfram von Eschenbach's *Parzival* which itself holds many clues to the identity of the real Grail.

> *"And sore was the King we sorrowed - Then a magic herb we found, (Men say, from the blood of a dragon it springeth from out of the ground,) with the stars, and the wind, and the heaven, close-bound, doth it win circling hour, And the moon draweth near to her changing, The herb might our grief have aided - Yet its magic we sought in vain."*

We are not searching in vain. The secret is now ours for the taking. Finally we know what the Grail is. It is the sacred mixing bowl, a skull cup, wherein was mixed the blood and venom of the snake to produce the healing Elixir of Life. This venom and blood mixture has now been proven by modern science to enhance and boost the immune system and thereby help us to fight off disease - it helps us to live longer and more healthy lives.[3]

Chapter 2 Sources:

The Righteous Teachers

American Bible Society, *The Holy Bible*, 1850

Collins', *The Holy Bible*, 1839

Josephus F, *The Complete Works*, Trans William Whiston, John E. Potter and Company Ltd,

Schonfield H, *The Essene Odyssey*, Element, 1993

Schonfield H, *The Passover Plot*, Element, 1993

Murphy T. W & Hopkins M, *Rosslyn – Guardians of the Holy Grail*, Element, 1999

Baigent M & Leigh R, *The Dead Sea Scrolls Deception*, Corgi, 1994

The Gospel of Thomas,
 http://www.misericordia.edu/users/davies/thomas/Trans.htm

Wilson I, *Jesus – The Evidence*, Weidenfeld and Nicholson, 1994

Olsen O, Editor, *The Temple 1 and 2*

Olsen O, Editor, *The Templar Papers*, New Page Books, 2006

Sinclair - The Mystery of the Name

A private letter & photocopied historical notes from Niven Sinclair dated 25th March 2003

Collins, Welsh Dictionary

P. Steele, T. Smart, *Encyclopedia of British History.*

Wace *Roman de Rou*

M. Baigent, R. Leigh and H. Lincoln, *The Holy Blood and the Holy Grail*

Farmer, *The Oxford Dictionary of Saints,*

The King Arthur Code References:

1   Harold Bayley. *The Lost Language of Symbolism* - Volume 2. 1912

2   Lorraine Evans. *Kingdom of the Ark.* 2000

3   Philip Gardiner with Gary Osborn. *The Serpent Grail*, Watkins, 2005

Chapter 3

The Templar Beauceant
By Oddvar Olsen

One of the main purposes of the Beauceant was as a rallying point for the Templars on the battlefield. And its importance can be understood when reading the Templar Rule. It was almost regarded a sacred object with a spirit of its own, having a number of clauses informing the brethren of the Temple of its use and purposes. The Tempar Rule as we know it today through Henri de Curzon's grand work of 1886 and later through J. M. Upton-Ward's book *'The Rule of the Templars'* was not a homogenous work but had evolved over 150 years, almost as long as the lifespan of the Knights Templar. The Beauceant significance throughout the Rule is very clear.[1]

The Rule dictates that up to ten serving Templar brothers could be appointed to guard the Beauceant and its bearer, who could be the Under Marshal, Marshal, Seneschal or Commander of Knights. Each squadron should also possess a Beauceant. If a brother showed any disregard or used it as a weapon, the perpetrator would be put in irons and heavily punish or even expelled from the order. To give a few examples from the Templar Rule:

When there is war and the brothers are lodged in an inn or established in camp, and the alarm is raised, they should not leave without permission, until the banner is taken out; and when it is taken out they should all follow it as soon as possible...(160)
... and these brothers should overwhelm their enemies all round the banner, to the best of their ability, and they should not leave or go away, rather they should stay as near to the banner as they can, so

73

that, if necessary, they may assist it. And the other brothers may attack in front or behind, to left and right, and wherever they think they can torment their enemies in such a way that, if the banner needs them they may help it, and the banner help them, if necessary. (164)

And if it happens that the Christians are defeated, from which God save them, no brother should leave the field to return to the garrison, while there is a piebald banner raised aloft; for if he leaves he will be expelled from the house for ever. And if he sees that there is no longer any recourse, he should go to the nearest Hospital or Christians banner if there is one, and when this or the other banners are defeated, henceforth the brother may go to the garrison, to which God will direct him. (168)

...if a brother leaves his banner and flees for fear of the Saracens; (he will be expelled from the house)" (232)

(Each number denotes clauses in Upton-Ward's *'The Rule of the Temlars'*, 2002)

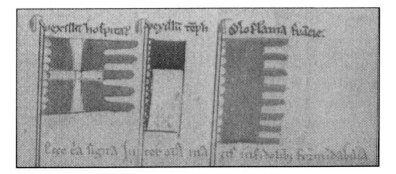

The first use of the Beauceant was according to C. G Addison as the Templars prepared to attack Damascus. Unfortunately, Addison does not mention on which source he drew, but relates it as follows; *'Shortly after King Louis arrived, accompanied by the new Master of the Temple, Everad des Barres (1146); and the Templars now unfolded for the first time the red cross banner in the field of battle. This was a white standard made of woollen stuff, having in the centre*

of it the red-blood cross, granted by Pope Eugenius. The two monarchs, Louis and Conrad, took the field, supported by the Templars, and laid siege to the magnificent city of Damascus...'[2]

On page 50 he quotes Cardinal de Vitry, Bishop of Acre (de Vitry often accompanied The Templars on various occasions); *'...They carry before them...to battle, a banner, half black and white, which they call Beau-seant, that is to say, in the Gallic tongue, Bien-seant, because they are fair and favourable to the friends of Christ, but black and terrible to his enemies'.*[3] (MaCoy gives the date 1191 for this event)

The important position of Beauceant-bearer was called the Balcanifer. Matthew Paris, lists one of the Balcanifer's as Reginald d'Argenton. Together with the Balcanifer a number of knights and squires were sworn to protect their banner and never loose it to the enemy. D'Argenton is described as a man who preformed *prodigies of valour*. After William de Montserrat, Preceptor of Antioch tried to besiege a fortress in the neighbourhood of Antioch, where; *'a hundred knights of the Temple and three hundred cross-bowmen were slain together with many secular warriors, and a large number of foot soldiers', still 'd Argenton was disabled and covered with wounds, yet he unflinchingly bore the Beauceant, or war-banner, aloft with his bleeding arms into the thickest of the fight, until he at last fell dead upon a heap of his slaughtered comrades'.*[4] (MaCoy gives the date 1229 for this event)

Robert MaCoy in his enlarged version of C.G Addisons, *History of Knights Templars* describes three different medieval flags:

'The PENNON, the ensign of knightly rank, small pointed, or swallow-tailed, and charged with a badge or other armorial device, was displayed by a Knight upon his own lance as his personal ensign.

The BANNER, square or oblong in form, larger than a pennon, and charged with a complete coat of arms, was ensign of the sovereign, prince, noble, or Knight-Banneret, and also of entire force attached to his person, and under his immediate command.

The STANDARD, introduced about the middle of the Fourteenth Century, large, of a great length (its size varying with the owner's rank), appears to have been adapted for military display rather than for any specific significance and use in war. Except in Royal standards the English standard had the Cross of St George next to the staff, and rest of the field displayed various badges, sometimes accompanied with a motto.'[5]

The Saracens had their banner as well, Masonic historian MaCoy in his *History of Knights Templars*, describes the banner of the

Saracen thus: *'...The spirit of Saracenic war, in which this defence was made, had its exemplar in the day long afterwards, when the black banner of Tamberlane was hung out – the first day's white, meaning (that the enemy should) surrender; the second's red, meaning blood of a few; the third's black, meaning universal destruction!'*[6] Interestingly the Templars chose the same colour scheme for their battle-flag. Macoy not unsurprisingly points out about the Beauceant: *'The idea is quite an oriental one, black and white being always used among the Arabs metaphorically, in the sense above described. Their customary salutation is, May you be white, i.e. may you be happy'.*[7]

The origin of the Beauceant is somewhat unclear. As the Rule uses the term *Banner* for the Templar Beauceant in most instances, this may suggest that it actually was adopted from a Coat of Arms of a sovereign, prince, noble or Knight-Banneret (see p...). I have searched the connected families to the founding Templar Knights in hope to find a Coat of Arms that would resemble the black and white banner of the Templars, although as of yet, to no avail.

As the Beauceant was black and white, it has also been named *the piebald* in a similar terminology used to describe a dappled horse. The Banner had a rectangular shape, two-thirds black on the top, white beneath, sometimes with a red cross, as described by C. G. Addison. The three images included in this article are all showing different variations of the Beauceant. This may indicate that a variety of banners were in use, however most Templar scholars generally agree that the predominantly black banner is the more authentic. Symbolically - white usually represents the good and pure; black symbolises death and the darker aspects of life.

As good Christians an inviting question summons: why did the Templars use a predominately black banner and even raised the black over the pure white? This does not correspond with Christian allegory. The Cathars and Gnostics believed mankind was living in a world full of evil (black), is it this that the Templar Beauceant depicts as well?

The Knights Templar Labyrinth at Chartres Cathedral - France
By Terence F. Dick

Is there more to the intricate labyrinth than just a pathway of penance for pilgrims making a visionary journey to Jerusalem?

The intricate pattern of a circular labyrinth on the pavement below the great rose window in the nave of Chartres Cathedral in France is said to be a creation of the Knights Templar - an order of dedicated warrior monks founded in 1118 to protect pilgrims travelling on their way to the Holy Land. The Templars are associated with the symbol of the circle because of their desire to emulate the circular plan of the great Christian basilicas in Jerusalem. People have for centuries used the labyrinth as a means for meditation, or even perhaps to embark on a thoughtful journey of penitence. Some have even stated that it has lifted them to some higher spiritual plane. But it also bares a very distinctive name, called the 'Chemin de Jerusalem' (Road of Jerusalem). Could there be something more to the labyrinth than just simply a road for spiritual contemplation?

By taking a much closer look at its construction and seeing how it was put together, I discovered that the designer had for some reason placed inside the labyrinth an extra special feature. I am now a retired engineer, but in the past, the study of intricate drawings had become a way of life, so I went about my examination based on those past experiences.

I have provided drawings that show the results of my findings, which I hope, will make it easier for you to understand. At first sight the labyrinth would appear to represent a typical Christian symbol, this is because it contains four arms or quadrants that seem to represent a very large cross, this may of course indeed be true, but if you take a much closer look another feature suddenly becomes more apparent. Examine very closely the four quadrant divisions and see how the labyrinth path has been apportioned, especially how it spans out around the four quadrants. Notice that each portion or section of the pathway will either span over one quadrant, or over two quadrants. It never spans over three quadrants, this rule remains constant throughout the entire pathway - whether it is near the centre of the labyrinth or out towards the edge. (To understand how a path section is determined and what the two types of spanning examples mean, make a close study of the Labyrinth Drawing No.1.)

Because all sections of the labyrinth pathway are covered by this strict rule I have assigned to them two simple numerical values. I have assigned a number **(1)** where one section of path length spans over one quadrant at 90 degrees of arc, and a number **(2)** where one section of path length spans over two quadrants at 180 degrees of arc. (Trace your finger around the blank drawing of Labyrinth Drawing No.2. and discover for yourself how these numbers, and the system of spanning actually works.)

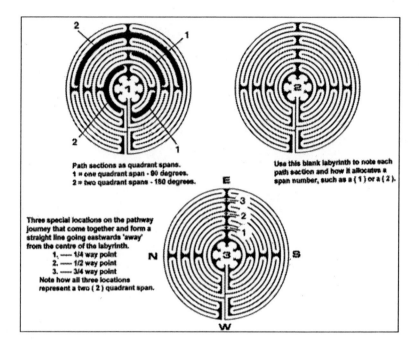

Path sections as quadrant spans.
1 = one quadrant span - 90 degrees.
2 = two quadrant spans - 180 degrees.

Use this blank labyrinth to note each path section and how it allocates a span number, such as a { 1 } or a { 2 }.

Three special locations on the pathway journey that come together and form a straight line going eastwards 'away' from the centre of the labyrinth.
1. ⎯⎯ 1/4 way point
2. ⎯⎯ 1/2 way point
3. ⎯⎯ 3/4 way point
Note how all three locations represent a two { 2 } quadrant span.

The number of pathway sections spanning the entire labyrinth around all of its four quadrants are **31**. To examine these sections more closely I have lifted the entire pathway out of the labyrinth and displayed it as you see it below in a straight line. Here you can see from the start position the first path section, or span, assigned as a (**1**), then by continuing on to the end of the line, or to the centre of the labyrinth and final path section, or span, which is also assigned as a (**1**).

Start - 1122112121211212121121212112211 - Centre = 31 path sections

|

middle of path

What strikes you immediately is the extraordinary patterning of the numbers. Notice how the path construction numbers start, and then end the same way beyond the middle position of the pathway. By placing a finger at both ends of the line begin tracing the same numbers towards the middle until you arrive at a central number 2, this is now the middle of the pathway but not the centre of the labyrinth. Notice also in the number line how certain numbers due appear to have grouped together, beginning with a 11221 then 1212121, then another 1212121, then another 1212121, ending with 12211. These five separate groups combined make the entire number line. These groupings will play a major role in an astonishing transformation of the entire labyrinth. Another interesting feature is that all the number 2s found in the three 1212121 sequence - add up to nine in total, could they have some special meaning for the nine founder members of the Knights Templar?

With the line of 31 path section numbers I have now applied a very simple numerical projection, something we are familiar with whenever we look at any graph type construction. The line of numbers have been projected vertically as blocks to the power of their numerical values - 1 or 2. You can see immediately how the line of blocks do resemble some kind of fortified wall. (Take a special note of the projected wall illustration which shows all 31 path sections taken from the labyrinth).

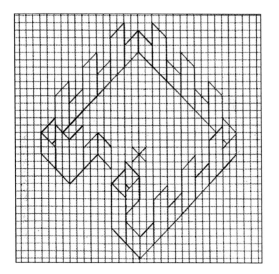

At this point I suddenly realised that something extraordinary was taking place. Could the double numbers placed in the line indicate some kind of angular feature? The only way to discover this was to cut out a small model of the line projection and make an angle where the double numbers appeared. Now, from what was once a labyrinth circle the line of blocks have suddenly transformed it into a perfect square. Then by creating further angles at each end where the (1122) 1 double number was located a large gateway structure has also presented itself. Could this small hidden image of a fortified enclosure possibly represent some kind of microcosm concerning the Temple area on the Temple Mount in Jerusalem that was once the headquarters of the Knights Templar during the middle ages?

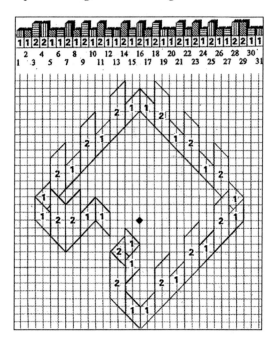

Take a special look at the provided isometric drawing that has projected the image into three dimensions, here you can see all the end results. It shows 31 path sections as individual panel pieces all connected together to make the four walls, each panel is numbered with a 1 or a 2 indicating its projected value. This amazing formation has produced two noticeable tower type structures that appear to flank this huge gateway, with some kind of vestible set deep inside the gate area.

As a travelling pilgrim you would enter into a labyrinth, not from the edge but halfway down towards the centre. You immediately turn left by making your way around the first path section, but as you walk along each section you are in fact visiting each invisible section of a wall, until you finally arrive approaching from the right, back to the centre. The beginning and the centre of the labyrinth have in effect been joined together as part of the exit and entrance of the gate. The central number 2 in each of the three groups of 121(2)121 - if you trace each one carefully around the path of the labyrinth – they all line up in a central line facing eastwards from the centre towards the altar. (See the Labyrinth Drawing No.3) They in turn represent a central position in each of the three walls. To achieve these stunning results it must surely have taken some extraordinary mathematical genius to plan out all the different angles and locations. It is staggering to think that a square image of this kind could have been created and hidden in secret, inside this circular labyrinth.

My own view is that this hidden structure the Templars have left behind is quite possibly a very special microcosm of the Temple courtyard enclosure with its large gate that was once their headquarters that surrounded the Al-Aqsa Mosque up to 1187 - as noted from a Gouache on paper drawing taken from the Muraqqa Album. This cleverly contrived structure has miraculously produced a symbolic protective temple wall barrier - albeit an invisible one - on four sides of the Chartres Labyrinth. Could it be that those central number 2s which face east, and also are the quarter, halfway, and three quarter positions located on the pathway journey, represent three important places inside

Solomon's Temple, such as the three rooms: 1. The Porch or vestible, (ulam); 2.The main room or Holy Place, (hekhal); and 3. the Holy of Holies (devir), where the sacred Ark once rested? Or is there perhaps a Christian meaning that refers to each of these three locations? One thing is really certain, and that is these points are destined to be visited in turn by every traveller as they walked around through all the sections of the labyrinth. The actual centre of the labyrinth then must surely be only part of the return journey - as noted by the identical numerical pattern seen at the beginning and end of the number line. The gate certainly is without doubt an amazing structure, could it possibly be The Golden Gate that marked a grand entrance into the Temple courtyard area? It is of course invisibly located inside the western door of the Cathedral as you enter onto the labyrinth. Is there be perhaps a moment of great expectation as you pass through this invisible gate onto a sacred area. That is if you know what the hidden secret is, in the labyrinth?

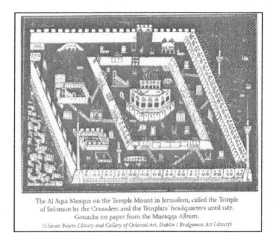

The Al Aqsa Mosque on the Temple Mount in Jerusalem, called the Temple of Solomon by the Crusaders and the Templars' headquarters until 1187. Gouache on paper from the Muraqqa Album.
(Chester Beatty Library and Gallery of Oriental Art, Dublin / Bridgeman Art Library)

A certain John of Wurtzburg writing in 1160 - 1170 says, "When you descend to the main street, there is a great gate through which one may enter the great courtyard of the Temple. On the right side, toward the south, is a palace which they say Solomon built".

As an engineer, I am greatly impressed by the construction techniques employed by the Templar designer who has marked out the design - it truly is a masterpiece. You begin to understand his extraordinary ability as he went about his work. To propose and demonstrate a Templar mystery is a rare experience, and yet even now I am still unsure whether all the details have been thoroughly covered and translated as many other possibilities still keep coming to mind. Chartres Cathedral is clearly a remarkable 'Golden Book' with much more to be read. But as for the labyrinth, what other secrets are still yet to be found there?

Royston Cave – What Exactly is it?
By Sylvia P. Beamon, MA (Cantab)

The town of Royston is situated at the northernmost point of Hertfordshire where the two ancient roads, the Roman Ermine Street/Ashwell Street and the Icknield Way, cross at its centre. It is directly on the Meridian Line today. The town is post-Domesday and did not become a settlement until an Augustinian Priory was founded there during the 12th century. The town straddled, and still does straddle, the boundaries of five parishes in the two counties of Hertfordshire and Cambridgeshire. Once it was granted its market charter by Richard I in 1189, a market was set up every Wednesday at the crossroads. This enabled the town to flourish as an economic centre for its surrounding area.

What, one might ask, makes Royston any different from all the rest? One remarkable feature sets this town apart from any other place in Britain and indeed the world, as far as is known, * and that feature is the Royston Cave. It could be argued that to describe it as a 'Cave' is not entirely accurate but no one has yet found a better name for it. Cut out of middle horizon chalk, it is not a natural cave in the geological sense and was excavated by man, yet it is completely underground. Its original function and by whom it was created is still open to debate.

This unique, small man-made bottle-shaped underground cavern, some 30 feet [9 m] high and 18 feet [5.5 m] in diameter appears to be two- storied, lying above and below a reticulated frieze, but whether it started out with Neolithic men digging a shaft in their search for flint, the seeking of water, or the start of a simple cellar then enlarged downwards is anyone's guess.

The cave was discovered in 1742, purely by accident by workmen constructing a bench for women in the butter market. Whilst hammering a post into the ground it went straight through the 'eye' of a millstone. On lifting this millstone a rubble-filled shaft was uncovered, later to be called the North shaft. First a young boy was lowered on a rope, then a 'thin' man who both reported there were one or two chambers below. When it was emptied of 'garden mould' the walls were found to be covered with engravings of saints, recognised as St. Katherine, St. Lawrence, St. Christopher, St. George or St. Michael, plus Crucifixion scenes. And included were various unusual signs and symbols. Little was found in the infill, a human skull and one or two other bones, a piece of brass lacking any inscription and a few pieces of medieval pottery. Later a seal with a single fleur de lis design on it was handed in. Serious archaeology at that time was non-existent and the whereabouts of the material, if kept, is unknown. The most intriguing aspect by far is that the decorated walls with carvings sculpted from the chalk were once coloured, and range in content from the pagan to the religious, thus posing the most tantalising questions as to its origins and uses. Doubtless, this structure has been used for many different purposes throughout the centuries, however the consensus of opinion is that the lower chamber is presumed to have been used at least as an oratory at some time.

There is a second shaft within the structure called the East shaft, perhaps a former air shaft. It was blocked up when the Cave was found. There is another opening, right at the very top of the tiled dome, which is grilled to allow air to circulate. When in the Cave daylight percolates down and people can be seen walking over the grille as it lies in the blocked-paved pathway above.

There were three former main Cave theories. Between 1743 and 1746, the Rev. Dr. William Stukeley (known as the first 'field archaeologist' in our country who travelled around and drew what he saw at various historical sites) wrote two books. He thought that the Cave was a chapel carved by no less a person than Lady Roisia de Vere, wife of Geoffrey de Mandeville, the first Earl of Essex, depicting her family history in the 12th century. For a few years it is likely that she and her family did live at the Newselles Manor House, Herts, just four miles away from Royston.

The Rev. Charles Parkin wrote two malicious books in answer to Stukeley's books and concluded it was a hermit's cell and oratory. Sometimes hermits did help travellers and one may have lived here for a while to point people in the four cardinal directions. Parkin also maintained that a Hundred Court had been held here since King Alfred the Great, but there is no firm evidence.

Joseph Beldam, in the mid 1800s, was the third antiquarian writer and his conclusions were: that the Cave was first formed by means of shafts, either by British or Roman-British men BC, then later used as a Roman columbarium. This idea is unlikely as there are not enough niches in the walls to accept cinerary urns. Next, he thought it received most of its decoration about the crusading period and then, if not before, it was converted into a Christian oratory to which a hermit was probably attached in the 16th century. He felt it was filled in about 1540 at the time of the Reformation.

It was from Beldam's comments that the author of this paper initially went some steps forward into the crusading aspect. The Knights Templar were a Crusading Order (1118 - 1308). A good description of them is that they were 'monks of war'. They lived as monks under their own 'Rule' devised by the Benedictine prelate St Bernard, the holy abbot of Clairvaux, France, yet fought as soldiers when called to arms to fight in the Crusading battles in Palestine. Much land, carefully documented, was given to the brethren all over Europe, including Britain. Several local landowners also donated land to them. There were Templar houses at Cambridge and Baldock, which were not as important as preceptories [larger establishments similar to monasteries] as at Hitchin, Herts, Duxford and Shingay-cum-Wendy, Cambs., all these places only a few miles from Royston. Smaller parcels of land were received from Reed, Whittlesford and Royston. The exact whereabouts of the land in Royston is not known but its existence is recorded in the Papers and Letters of King Henry VIII, Vol 15, 1540.)

Baldock, Herts. is 9 miles [14.4 km] away from Royston, was a Templar created market town. Their land around economically supported them during peaceful times. Every week, probably no more than two or three Templars (those who were artisans and wore brown garments with red crosses on them) travelled to Royston for the weekly market where they sold produce from their farms, no doubt including butter, cheese, wine from their vineyards at Weston and leather goods. It is possible that an upper storey of the Cave was used as a store for market goods. It would have been a suitable cool environment to keep dairy food cool, particularly in the summer months.

There were a lot of disputes, including court cases, between the Templars and the Prior of Royston who was in charge of the market - fortunately recorded between 1199 - 1254. Because the Templars were favourites of the English monarchy, they did not have to pay stallage in markets, and this monetary dispensation certainly did not make them popular with either the Prior or other market stallholders. On one occasion the Prior took 37 shillings from them, a considerable sum then, which he had to return to them following their appeal to the King. The author has hypothesised that after this particular dispute, the Prior probably denied the Templars use of the Priory church for prayers; therefore it became necessary to create a little chapel for themselves. Every day they had to say regular prayers, as well as 40 obits for the dead [obits were prayers for their dead brethren and those who had died in the Crusading wars].

Some churches built by the Templars were distinctive in shape, circular on the outside and a few, octagonal within, perhaps copied from the Church of the Holy Sepulchre, their esteemed shrine in Jerusalem. Although the Royston Cave does not look exactly the same, it is circular in the bottom area and does have a raised octagonal ledge carved out of the chalk floor close to the walls. Even though the shape is not obvious1 now since time and wear has given it an appearance of being almost circular, a resistively test of 1972 indicated that the floor area was cut originally in a square, then another square was cut in between the four sides to form the octagon. This ledge or podium may have been used as a seat, except it is rather low. Another explanation could be that it was used to kneel upon to say prayers.

It is exceedingly fortunate that both Stukeley and Beldam,

over a hundred years apart, drew what they saw when they visited the Cave and put the illustrations in their books. A couple of large lumps and other smaller bits of chalk from the carvings have fallen off since. By close examination of their drawings it is possible to determine how they were before, although they were not all completely accurate even then. Firstly, they were sketched, and afterwards redrawn a lot from memory. Of course, photography did not exist and the light poor from candles and lanterns. (Parkin allegedly never visited the Cave but copied Stukeley's drawings to illustrate his own books. Stukeley's drawings remain in the Bodleian Library, Oxford)

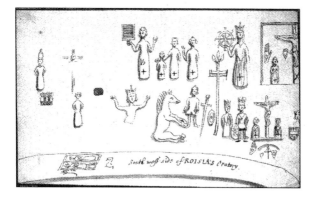

Dating of the carvings is difficult, and can only be done stylistically at present. For example, St. Christopher is carrying the Christ Child on his shoulder. He is sculpted in relief in the 13th style and correctly placed on a North wall by an entrance as would be expected in an ordinary church. The main altar is a floriated cross. This is another dating point and seen only up to the 14th century in other works of medieval art. But it is on the West wall instead of East to face Jerusalem as occurs in Christian churches. Why? Perhaps it is because the main altar in the Holy Sepulchre Church in Jerusalem lies at West too. It did not need to face East there because it was already there in the Holy City.

The large Crucifixion scene, lying just beyond St. Katherine [clockwise] to whom the chapel was dedicated, shows Jesus on the Cross, with his mother Mary on the left and Apostle John, on the right. This arrangement is also an indication that it was carved after 1200 because Christ's feet appear crossed, his body turned to the right and the two figures either side stand upright. In all probability if it had been cut later in the middle of the 1300s, then Mary should have been seen half fainting and looking towards her Son. At the feet of Christ is a symbol, the St. Andrew's Cross, and it is telling the onlooker that Jesus was the second person of the Trinity [God, the Father, God, the Son and God, the Holy Spirit]. What is most unusual is that there are hands with hearts, double hearts, even a triple heart, all lying within the actual scene.

Another symbol should be noted, the ancient Hebraic quaph, resembling an axe head or a cross with a loop over the top. It can be seen three times around the walling at the bottom of the Cave and once in the dome. This symbol, which the French claim is Templar, explains that the Templars were a dichotomy, and had two functions, as mentioned before, firstly monks and secondly soldiers but linked together. Some Templars including Jacques de Molay the Grand Master were imprisoned in the Tour de Coudray, Chateaux de Chinon, France on suppression of the Order, and a panel of graffiti including this symbol is attributed to these prisoners, prior to them being removed from prison and burnt at the stake.

It would not be too surprising to find a small Templar establishment, including a chapel, at the Royston cross-road because the Knights Templar order initially undertook to help pilgrims on their way to Jerusalem, the Templars first raison d'etre, and these two main roads were well used. The Templars were to take care of the Crown jewels in their Temple Church in London and became bankers. They were responsible for moving large sums of money throughout England and abroad equivalent of today's security guards. As Royston Cave itself does not seem to have been recorded it might have been deliberate, because the Templars chose to keep it as a 'safe house' so the general public did not know where they kept valuables from time to time. And there is always the suggestion that Templars held secret meetings where they carried out certain heretical practises, the forerunners of Freemasonry. After the French king Philip le Bel wrote to the English King Edward II asking him to get rid of the Templars. During a three-month period taken up with exchange of letters, quite a number of Templars quietly disappeared to Scotland. And the road from Dover, London, passes through Royston, and via York leads to Scotland! Who knows what the answer is?

To conclude the author is of the opinion the Cave was probably no more than a simple cellar to store market goods brought to Royston by the Templars from Baldock. The usual medieval day was six miles walking or carting with horse and cart, marketing all day, then a return home – a total of 12 miles. Quite a long day. But Baldock is 9 miles away, which would have added a further six miles to the day and suggest that the men stayed overnight each week. If, through the dispute with the Prior the brethren were unable to use the Priory Church and creating an oratory became almost a necessity, then these Templars would have had time to decorate the oratory below.

Addenda:

The author has lived in Royston since 1961 and, although fascinated by the Cave, was frustrated by the dearth of written evidence, and devoted 25 years to exhaustive research in the hope of finding the elusive answers. She travelled far and wide in Britain and on the Continent in her efforts to solve the enigma of the carvings, establishing in the process a probable link with the Knights Templar Order. To this end, she has written and published several highly successful, articles, pamphlets and booklets culminating in the definitive book published in 1992. These alone have provided a major contribution to heightening public awareness of the Cave, not only in Royston, but also worldwide, and of the necessity to preserve and protect this unique Listed Grade I English monument for future generations.

Furthermore, because of the inevitable chalk-pilling through temperature changes in the Cave and damage caused by constant flooding, it is vital that there is an accurate record published and a laser photogrammetry survey for posterity.

* There are known to be caves in the Gaza strip claimed by Beldam to be similar in shape to that of the Cave, but of course, this is not a possible avenue to pursue at the present unstable time. There is also a small medieval cavity in Sloup Castle in the Czech Republic, which is worthy of mention. It does have some engravings but not as splendid as those at Royston.

The Green Man, St George and the Templars
By Paul Broadhurst

Medieval woodcut from Malory's Morte d'Arthur, *linking St George with the Arthurian mythos.*

When we strip away the modern association of St George from the more unsavoury elements of unthinking nationalism, it soon becomes clear that the illustrious saint has lost none of his timeless appeal in the hearts and minds of millions of people throughout the world. Wherever we travel, from the troubled lands of the Middle East to the remote regions of Russia and Central Europe, we find that he is still honoured as one of the timeless spiritual guides of humanity. He also presides over the great historical institutions like a guiding light, with his chapels and churches located at the very centres of power. Why, we may find ourselves asking, does this alleged Roman soldier martyred for his beliefs right at the beginning of the Christian era still exert such a powerful influence, especially as in 1969 the Vatican demoted him to the rather undignified status of a minor local saint?

The truth is that the long and glorious career of St George has been the target of a campaign of Church propaganda since the very beginning. Close examination of the available records can only lead to the conclusion that the Roman general who is said to have died for his Christian beliefs is unlikely to have ever existed, at least with the name George. Eusebius, the generally reliable chronicler and Bishop of Caeseria in whose province the martyrdom occurred, never even mentions him. It is only when that arch-manipulator Constantine the Great begins to rewrite history at the various councils of the early fourth century that George surfaces as a suitably heroic figure to lead the Holy War against paganism. In Constantine's New World Order the political and military need to create a state religion was imperative; the very existence of the Roman Empire was at stake.

When we begin to look at some of the other elements of the George myth a completely different picture begins to emerge. One of the most telling clues to the genuine mystery behind the George phenomenon is in the name itself. The word begins and ends with the root *Ge*. This is one of the oldest words known, occurring in Sumerian, Egyptian, Greek and Indo-European languages. It means *Earth*. Everyday words still in common use such as Ge-ology or Ge-ography show how persistent this root has been over at least the last six thousand years.

The etymology of *George* thus appears to show that he may originally have been an Earth-God connected with fertility, whose widespread worship in the ancient world was absorbed by Constantine's attempts to make early Christianity into an all-inclusive religion that would become a vehicle for Roman bureaucracy. To reinforce this view the Greek translation of the name means 'Earth-worker' or 'Tiller of the soil'. What has this got to do with a martyred soldier? The widespread appearance of St George in Mayday and other springtime folk rituals also appears to show that he was the presiding spirit of such festivities that have their roots in pre-Christian times. It begins to look as though George may have originally represented the fertile spirit of the Earth itself, the force that lies dormant in the winter and awakens each spring to bring renewed Life. His 'martyrdom' is that of the dying god who is resurrected each year, and on whose rebirth we are all dependent.

Many centuries after the supposed existence of the Roman St George a new element was grafted onto the myth that turned him into a dragon-slayer. This came about because of a story in Jacobus de Voragine's *The Golden Legend*, a compendium of the lives of the saints. Destined to become one of the best-selling books of all time it had a massive influence on the popular psyche, for in those days it was believed that such writings were the results of historical scholarship and not propaganda or mass mind-control through the media, as we might perhaps see it today. But Jacob was Bishop of Genoa, one of the great maritime trading and banking centres of the Knights Templar, a city dedicated to St George. Its foundation legend told of San Siro, who coaxed a troublesome draconic serpent from a well and banished it. Such legends were common throughout the pre-Christian world and it seems more than likely that Jacobus' grafting of the dragon legend onto that of St George was yet another exercise in bringing the pagan mythologies into line with the worship of the One True God. His idea worked brilliantly, for it blended the Dragon Lore of the Celtic world with the heroic knight of Christendom who fought for Truth and Justice.

It also, beyond its fairy-tale appeal to the common mind, alluded to a tradition that was well-known amongst the mystically-inclined Templars. This was the esoteric science of the Dragon Power of Nature, the Life-Force that animates the Earth, the Kundalini or fiery serpent power cultivated by mystics and those involved in the search for enlightenment, the essential root of evolving spiritual consciousness. It is today acknowledged that the Templars were deeply immersed in such spiritual quests, as the inheritors of their own native mysticism and also having learnt much from the Sufi masters at the great schools of Persia, the Holy Land and the rest of the Middle East. And so in one deft stroke, the archetypal image of St George as a dragon-slayer (that is, an enlightened being taming the spiritual force of the dragon) became a universally-recognisable symbol that was readily adopted by the Templars and their compatriots. It symbolised everything they stood for, and also made a profound statement to initiates that Christianity, Paganism and Islam were all derived from the same spiritual roots, whatever the political machinations of the time.

Much of these underground beliefs can be clearly seen in the buildings that were created in the great religious flowering of the 12th and 13th centuries, when a massive leap forward in architectural design accompanied one of the greatest waves of construction in history – the Gothic Revival. One of the most interesting motifs employed throughout this time was the ubiquitous foliate head known today as The Green Man. The significance of this image can hardly be overestimated, for throughout European churches and cathedrals it vastly outnumbers images of Christ. It is arguably the predominant image in ecclesiastical architecture of the period. Whilst some maintain it represents little more than the pagan spirit of vegetation, studies of the different styles (sometimes agonising as if in the throes of death, or depicted as a young virile male or even a new-born babe) indicate that it is a direct reference to the dying and rising god of pre-Christianity that was supplanted by the advent of Jesus Christ.

Green Man from Kilpeck Church, Herefordshire, surmounting a column whose base terminates in a serpent's or dragon's head.

These powerful connections between the Green Man and St George and the Dragon can be seen everywhere when we realise that medieval sculpture was a way of encoding information through the use of symbolic imagery. Few seem to have noticed how often these motifs are deliberately linked by those who designed the sculptures. There are literally thousands of examples. On the outside of Basle Minster in Switzerland is a dramatic representation of St George spearing a Dragon above an ancient doorway; he rises from a pedestal formed by the head of a Green Man. The message could hardly be plainer; the figure of St George on his white horse (a Celtic symbol of the Otherworldly regions) is firmly built upon the foundations of the Green Man; anyone passing through the portal to the Minster beyond is obliged to recognise that the powers of Nature and its cycles of death and rebirth are amongst the most powerful and transformative forces on Earth.

The Dragon, before it was demonised by the medieval Church to promote fear in a last-ditch attempt to destroy the lingering pre-Christian ways, was almost invariably a beneficent symbol of natural power. This esoteric understanding of the former Celtic Christian Church in many instances carried over into certain strands of later orthodox Christianity. Hundreds of churches and cathedrals have massive dragons carved over their entrances; they guard the site and imbue it with spiritual power. Some examples in Britain are Bristol, Manchester and Lincoln Cathedrals, the latter with a pair of very dramatic and wonderfully carved dragons over the West Door. These are the remnants of the original builders' understanding preserved in stone. The widespread Dragon legends that can be found in every land often refer to the dragons as dangerous and a threat to the local inhabitants; however, on examination one can clearly discern how much older legends have been adapted by Church propaganda to bring people under their control and inculcate fear of the old ways.

One of the many 'green dragons' in Rosslyn Chapel, often closely associated with the ubiquitous Green Man.

Those legends that still preserve the true, original flavour of these stories which come echoing down from prehistory frequently tell how the saint or holy man does not slay the dragon, but tames it through the power of prayer or magic. Some, like the Druid-like St Samson of Cornwall, even lived in the dragon's lair so that they could experience the natural power of the place so recently vacated by the beast itself. Many ancient festivals still have dragons as their central focus; wild, cavorting figures around which the local people dance with dervish-like energy. A great number of these dragon-worshipping festivities were banned by the Church who were intimidated by their power. One Vicar at Padstow in Cornwall tried to bribe the villagers with as much food and drink as they could consume if only they refused to indulge in the annual Mayday 'Obby Oss' ritual, which was notorious for its licentiousness. Not one complied. To this day one can still sense the sheer vivacity of such proceedings, and the genuine spirit of celebration at the rebirth of the spring god of fertility. The 'Oss', it has to be said, looks far more like a dragon than a horse, and of course St George, as the spirit of renewal, is a central figure in this and many other such celebrations. At Padstow he ritually 'dies' accompanied by an emotionally-charged and mournful song before suddenly the Oss suddenly leaps up, reborn at the same moment as St George.

Whilst the links between the Green Man and St George and the Dragon can be shown throughout the rituals of a bygone era, they can also be seen preserved in stone and wood in churches in both the West and East, where St George is often called by his Arabic name of *al Khidr*, literally *The Green One*. In Islamic tradition he leaves green footprints in the desert and appears spontaneously to those who earnestly seek spiritual guidance. The years spent by the Templars in the Holy Land, where they are known to have had intimate contacts with their Arabic counterparts, must have given them many further insights into the mystery. They soon adopted George as their patron saint, who, according to their own accounts, often appeared as a shining figure leading them to victory. They were convinced that it was through the saint's intercession that Richard the Lionheart won the Battle of Acre, and they wore a blue garter as a symbol of brotherhood, as was practised in the Sufic tradition. This was the origin of the Knights of the Noble Order of the Garter, which carried the mystical stream of thought right to the heart of

European society, where it blended seamlessly with the Arthurian mythos and the quest for enlightenment.

The returning Crusaders, and especially the Templars and their associated societies and brotherhoods, were instrumental in reinvigorating the religious impulse after the depredations of war and pestilence that had swept across Europe in the preceding centuries. A new vision was materialising, a revival of the eternal truths behind all religions. The incorporation of the Byzantine arch in the new Gothic architecture, the prevalence of the Green Man prominently displayed in churches and cathedrals and their knowledge of the true power of the Dragon was a powerful statement of the unity behind the various traditions. And because the Templars had become so wealthy and influential (which they must have thought at least partially due to their association with St George) they could leave messages for the future.

These messages can still be seen today, wherever they have survived the neglect or changing fashions of later centuries. One such place that has become a focus of attention due to the newfound interest in the mystical traditions of Templarism is Rosslyn Chapel, near Edinburgh. This 'arcane library of secrets' is literally covered in carvings that preserve in stone the wisdom of their beliefs, each symbol having been personally chosen by its builder the Grand Master William St Clair. Observers have noted that there are hundreds of Green Men adorning the chapel (but only one image of Christ). Yet what is equally intriguing is that there is also a fantastic collection of 'Green Dragons'; with foliage spilling out of their mouths just like their more human counterparts. Many of these Green Men and Dragons are directly linked together, as if they both represent different aspects of the same force of Nature.

Intertwined dragons at the base of the Apprentice Pillar at Rosslyn. Spirals of greenery issue from their mouths to show that 'green dragons' are at the very foundation of the natural world.

The famous 'Apprentice Pillar' has four intertwined Dragons at its base, with intricate spirals of foliage rising upwards. Many believe that this pillar represents the Tree of Life that links Heaven and Earth. If so, then the foundations of the Tree of Life are rooted in the Dragon power of Nature, with its endless rhythms determined by the seasonal nature of the dying and rising vegetation god. But just as the Green Man must die to be resurrected anew, the mystical adepts who laid all these images before us knew that the enlightened individual must also be reborn in like fashion. From this perspective, St George is in a sense each and every one of us, taming our dragons so we can aspire to the full consciousness of Nature and its eternal mysteries.

*The Kilpeck serpent or dragon stone, with its tongue drawing spiritual
energies from the earth; a message from the master masons that
churches depend on Nature for their power.*

The Cameley Head – An Enigma
By Juliet Faith

I had been researching the Knights Templar for some years, when last year I turned my attention to an infrequently mentioned Templar village, that of Templecloud in the parish of Cameley near Bristol and Bath in the South West of England.

I was initially drawn to the old church of St. James at Cameley, which was originally the only church at Templecloud, and therefore seemed an obvious starting point for my search. The church is largely 12th century Romanesque style. Romanesque art and architecture was at its peak in the 12th century, which has later become known as the 12th century Renaissance. At St James's church, apart from some intriguing wall paintings, a Romanesque 'beak head' was found, which is now located in the British Museum. As an object of timber it is unique as most surviving beak heads are of stone. It also suggests that skilled craftsmen were employed to work on Cameley church, probably because at some point in history the church belonged to the Romanesque Priory at Bath.

What really caught my attention however, was a carved, wooden, mans head on the west wall of the church. My first impression of it was its resemblance to the Templecombe panel painting which is reputedly Templar and has a carbon date 14 date of c 1280 A.D. Both these heads are life size, open mouthed with carbuncle eyes, bearded and long haired. The Cameley head has an interesting lozenge design as its border, which will be discussed later on. As I looked at this head, descriptions of 'heads' from the Templar confessions came flooding to me:

"On the day of his reception 'a certain head' had been placed on the alter of the chapel and he was told to adore it...It appeared to an effigy of a human face red in colour and as large as a human head. [1]

"At Carcassone two brethren agreed they had adored a wooded image called Baphomet"[2]

"Nearly all the brethren agreed the head was bearded and had long hair" [3]

Could this I wondered, be one of the four 'idols/icons' supposedly brought to England for safe keeping after the arrest of the Templar in France?

I immediately looked to the church guide for more information and found none. The new vicar, Rev Thorne of the Parish knew nothing. I turned to the 'Churches Conservation Trust', who owns the church. First of all I was told there was no mention of the 'head' in the 1960's inventory, then after more phone calls and two letters I was told that the head had been recorded as the head of a woman in a Nebuly headdress and was probably c 14th century.

A woman with beard!

From this point onwards I have been in touch with various academics and experts and each with somewhat different view! All that I have been able to ascertain is that the head is NOT an architectural piece i.e. a corbel or roof boss, and that it was probably designed to be viewed 'face on'. The date seemed to confound people, as did the exact purpose of the object. On 16th February 2006 however, Dr Michael Costen, retired professor from Bristol University came to view the head, much to my delight he tentatively suggested that the head is 12th century origin. And he thought it particularly interesting and important, although he was not prepared to make any connection with the Templars at this stage.

It is known that King John granted the lands at Cameley, Huntspill and Lundy to the Templars some time before 1203. The Hippisley estate map for Cameley Parish (1766) reveals some interesting field names such as 'Temple field', 'Inner Temple field' and 'outer Temple Field'. There is also a road in the village called Templar way.

A possible link between the Templars and the church is the fact that it is dedicated to St. James, the Great. St. James is the patron saint of pilgrims, his shrine being at Santiago de Compostela in Spain. St. James was one of the Templars preferred saints, and the knights guarded the pilgrim route to Compostela.

Less tangible evidence that could link Cameley Church to the

Templars is that like many other Templar churches, St James is not on a perfect east-west alignment. It is slightly to the North of east. This is known as Patronal Alignment, when a church is aligned to the position of the sunrise on the morning of the saint's day to whom the church is dedicated. [4]

Another interesting feature inside the church are some barely visible eight sided 'foliate' designs painted on the wall and known to date from the 12th century. These are reminiscent of designs used by the Templars as decoration within other churches and on some tombstones, such as in Garway, Llanmadoc and Kilmory.

The four sided lozenge design that forms the border of the head reminds me of the borders of some of the supposed copies of the face of the Turin Shroud from places such as Alexandria, Serbia and Moscow. These date from the 12th and 13th centuries and are known as the Mandylion.

The shroud of Turin was folded in such a way that only the face was left visible, being held in place by a lozenge pattern grid. This is thought to be the possible origins of the Mandylion Icon.

To date, I am still very much researching the history of the Templars at Templecloud and Cameley. I believe that a carbon 14 dating of the head is due to take place autumn/winter this year; that at least will give a better clue as to whether this head had any contemporary connection with the Templars. My feeling is that it certainly did. In the meantime the village is slowly giving up its secrets – the quest goes on …

"And thus did the knights of the Temple vanish with their secret, in whose shadow breathed a lofty yearning for the earthly city. But the Abstracts to which their efforts aspired lived on, unattainable, un unknown regions…and its inspiration, more than once in the course of time, has filled those spirits capable of receiving it"[5]

The Cameley Head – An update
By Juliet Faith

"The visible image portrays an invisible truth."
Church text 1000 A.D.

In issue 9 of *The Temple*, I wrote an article about a strange carved wooden head that I had 'discovered' at the small C12th church in the village of Cameley in Somerset. My suggestion was that perhaps this head had once belonged to the Knights Templar as they had been in possession of land and property at Cameley during the 1200's.

I also said that a carbon 14 dating was going to take place to try and date the head, and identify the wood from which it is carved. It was understood that providing there was no cost to them, the Trust that own the church would agree to a sample of wood from the head being sent to the lab at Oxford for this purpose.

Sadly, even though the necessary funds were secured, the Trust have recently removed the head from public view, and as far as can be ascertained at present, the C14 dating, and a possible dendrochronological report will not be forthcoming.

This unfortunate turn of events has not in any way prevented continuing interest in the Cameley head, and all the interested parties still hope that one day a scientific study will be possible.

I believe that this is of particular importance because a very rare Romanesque beak-head was found at the same church which is believed to be the only surviving wooden Romanesque beak-head in Britain, making it very important and rare.

The beak head is c12th, and is carved from oak, it is currently held by The British Museum, although it is NOT on public display.

There are many of us who believe that the man's head could be of an equally early date, and as such, would be of equal, if not greater importance.

In my previous article I suggested the possibility that the head may have been one of the 'Idols' of the Knights Templar, which added fuel to the fire of condemnation of the order at the time of their suppression. I still hold to this belief.

The Templar's reputedly had an 'Idol' in each province, I suggest these objects of veneration were secreted away just prior to the suppression of the order, which would have allowed them to survive until the present day.

At Templecombe in Somerset, there is a similar 'head', which takes the form of a panel painting. This head has been dated to 1280 A.D. a time when the Templar's had their main South West preceptory at Templecombe.

Could it be that the Head at Cameley originally served the same function as the one from Templecombe, but was from another preceptory, possibly Bristol?

What these heads both have in common is that they represent a bearded male, with long hair, staring eyes, a long nose and an open mouth. Both images are 'cut off' at the neck and despite their present association with churches, neither one has a halo therefore is not an obvious religious artefact.

It is my opinion (and I am still continuing my research on this,) that both images are in fact Holy Face's, and may have been based on the image of the face on The Shroud of Turin, which itself has no halo.

There are other similar images at shrines in Europe, and these are hidden away from the public gaze. Ian Wilson, author and expert on *The Turin Shroud has* made a very interesting study of these images in his book *'Holy Faces Secret Places,'* he has drawn some startling conclusions.

For my part, the Holy Faces that Professor Wilson has illustrated in his book bear an astonishing resemblance to both the

Cameley Head, and the Templecombe panel painting.

In our own research, my colleague Clive Wilkins and I have consulted with several 'experts' on mediaeval art, architecture and sculpture, and whilst none can positively verify the purpose and origin of the Cameley Head, some of their suggestions point to the same conclusions as we have reached. These are: The head was an object of devotion; It has clearly been 'looked after', and escaped destruction during the reformation; It was NOT an architectural piece; the lozenge trellis border which frames it was probably gilded, the lozenge had its own symbolic and mystical associations. Most experts conclude that it needs to be dated.

Finally, returning to the Knights Templar, could it be that in reality the strange head that the knights were accused of venerating was in reality an image of Christ based upon the face of the shroud of Turin? I leave you with the words of Audrey Dymock Herdsman from Templecombe, writing after the discovery of the Panel Painting in 1957:

"...it tells us of the sort of thing they (The Templars) did in fact venerate, treasure, and hide from their persecutors. Sadly they could not tell the courts of these possessions without putting them at risk, and the strange survival of this painting to the present day pleads eloquently for their integrity."

Templar Hunting in the Czech Republic
Royston Cave, Herts. and Sloup, Ceska Lipa, Cz.
By Stephen Andrews

Prague is the most photogenic place. At each corner another spired turret or a sun burned painter. This home of Kafka and alchemy is now so accessible that it is a must for the Templar tourist, among others. So here is another signpost from the journey – on the journey.

Our trip began with the intention of comparing the possibly Templar underground workings in the Ceska Lipa region of the Czech Republic with those of the Cave at Royston in Hertfordshire. We were going to feel the ambience and observe in detail the confines of the underground cave at Sloup, in an attempt to reach a view on whether they are in some way connected by religious, sacred or other factors. More especially we were trying to find whether the Knights Templar might have been responsible for the mysterious carvings in either or both.

It is great to move half way across Europe in a three and a half hour flight. It gives you a different perspective. As you sweep in from the skies of Western Europe and see the land below bathed in spring sunshine you might possibly see the vastness of the Central European land mass, if only in your mind's eye. Only then when your host reminds you that (even with the good weather you are enjoying) *"an anticyclone can whip up snow from any direction"* do you get a true impression of the exposed nature of your location/destination. There is little between you and the Urals or for that matter Siberia. Then and only then are you prepared for the dawning awareness that there would have been very little between you and the Prusses and the other warlike tribes from the north. The Turks would get as far as Hungary from the South and though held at arms length the Golden

Hordes from the East would get as far as Poland. Had this been 1207 not 2007 it would be a far less hospitable place – even in the sunshine.

So we have unexpectedly received our first message from the past - a sense of the importance of the discipline necessary amongst the knights of all the military orders to push out the boundaries of their European domains. Never mind the reasons, for now; the extent of their exposure must have been daunting. One can only imagine life behind stockades of timber - palisades erected until the stone Templestejn were completed. It must have required a degree of steel in their outlook and backbone – never mind in their hand. Uncertain times require a different approach to fortitude and (like the Roman soldier's worship of Mithras before) the Templars unswerving faith and strength seems to have come from their beliefs in rebirth and resurrection through Christ (?) and fortitude from Ss Lawrence and Catherine.

(St Lawrence was strung out on a griddle over a giant bar-be-cue and Catherine tied to her wheel for a similar purpose because they would not give in to their tormentors – both feature in the carvings of Royston but are there similar glimpses in Sloup too? - we will see.)

Prague rose up from a great big hole – a meteorite smashed its way into the earth about 1,000 million years ago. Apart from shifting things about a bit - to a depth of up to 30 kilometres, it cascaded moldavites – and other semi precious stones across the landscape. (These moldavites, once polished, have a green lustrous fire that seem to glow from within and are sometimes known as 'Grail Stones') After the top most 5 km, or so, of topsoil and rock was eroded away in the intervening periods; the landscape that we see today in Bohemia was left. Already weakened by the impact, the crust or mantle was susceptible along the damage line and volcanic plugs mark out the places where the fault existed. All around the fault line there were different deposits that people have been seeking out ever since.

The Russians exploited Uranium for their purposes during their stay in the Czech lands and still earlier miners took out Gold and Silver notably from the mines of Kutna Hora. Little wonder that these metals are present in the symbols and wealth of the city – the uranium was not so openly celebrated.

Our first sojourn with my host, guide and friend (Vlaclav - a Geologist, that knows of alchemy, art, archaeology and architecture and the green man too!) was spent in the tranquil surroundings of the Wallenstein renaissance gardens that are situated close to the Parliament buildings and the Malostranska underground station. They were created in 1535 for Ferdinand I. They are open from May to October, 10 am - 6 pm daily. The gardens are free and open to the public. Among the bronze statues of fawns, satyrs and virgins, haughty peacocks strode around – displaying their control over their environment and their peahens. In a *physic* garden this nearly flightless bird is perhaps an appropriate symbol – of the air; but doomed effectively to walk the earth forever. Then there is what can only be described as a semi circular wall of cemented grapes. It is in fact a construct that looks like Old Mother Shipton's cave - a clinker like material, ground down and applied to a brick wall to give the shape or form. Within the dried grey porridge exist a dark foreboding theme and fierce dragons and wonderful beasts peer out from the hand made stalactites and stalagmites. The romantic effect of this hanging petrified garden is to offer a balance - a counterpoint to the clean light airy formality of the garden and its paths – the grotto – a reminder of pain and horror that would have been just visible to the renaissance man and his guests as they sat in their pavilion enjoying the breezes and picking at dainty morsels.

The next day, after a cross-city drive and a walk in the park (where the ghosts of 1970s spy stories can be seen walking among the trees) our second day visit was to the wonder of Hvezda – the Star Palace (http://www.universutopia.net/note.asp?L=EN& note_id=55). The plasterwork ceilings are just amazing and the creatures of myth are so finely crafted you fancy that each could peck or bite you if you take your eyes from the beauty of the human form and the Green Men portrayed at every turn. In the vaulted basement (reminiscent of the round churches of Bjornholm) there is a detailed model of the battle of the 'White Mountain' so influential in the Catholic / Protestant history of Europe. But don't lose sight of the building form – as above –so below is explained and not for the last time in the Czech lands.

A good host doesn't tell you where to go or what to think but facilitates and augments. So it was when Vaclav suggested the journey to Mlada Boleslav. A 14th century castle with possibly earlier foundations sits on a hillside over-looking a bend in the river and a sugar factory. Among the castle buildings that may have been commenced from the 1050s is a wonderful example of what looked to be an older building that completed one side of the courtyard. Although Czech historians do not seemingly recognise Templar holdings, preferring to speak of the Johannite warrior monks that followed, there are still built styles that are of that certain time. The building for me had the hallmarks of a

Templar period building. Non-arched, flat, rubbed stone lintels over square window openings, the pitch of the roof and (peering inside) a brick filled vaulted ceiling holding up the first floor above. It looked *right* in its scale and form, a rustic version of other buildings that form part of recognised ranges of Templar buildings seen elsewhere in Europe. Maybe they were just old buildings of the *right* period. The date seemed correct, but it was perhaps its proximity to another strange Romanesque building that made the location more interesting.

In my Templar hunting, I am rarely drawn by a latter day title like 'Templ' and in Mlada Boleslav it proved to be a good rule again as the building known as Templ was based on a much older foundation. It was not a real temple nor was it 'Templar'– more a museum to the ancestors that had lived and died there in the sand-stone caves that lay beneath the current building. An audiovisual slide show cleverly explained how light penetrated the sandstone cave and shone about the ancestor's bones but sadly it is a *mock-up* of somewhere else. Never mind! - when you are outside you can see the cave entry points where the inhabitants of a thousand years had gained entry to their refuge in the cliff faces that form the river valley. Templ museum is sited on or over the 'ancient settlement' mentioned in the guided walk of the town.

Elsewhere in this museum of burials and bones was, for me, the sight of the town – a 11th –12th century sword was there 'shining' among the exhibits... I say shining in the sense that it stuck out. It could not shine really. It had an ellipse shaped pommel above a rusty handle and a rust eaten blade serrated by the harsh edge of time. A Norman / Viking / Templar / St John's Knight blade. Who knows? Who cares?! It was the same scale and form as those cut into the supposed Templar gravestones I have seen on Bute and elsewhere in the West of Scotland. Baigent and Leigh suggested that to safeguard their anonymity, even in death, only the Templars personalised sword would be incised on the grave top. Here was 7-800 years worth of proof that swords were of that size and shape. I worshipped in front of the sword for minutes until the boredom of my wife became palpable and we headed out of the Museum in search of sweet chocolate drinks. As we left the proprietor pointed out the Romanesque door and its special bar. This place had been secure for many years.

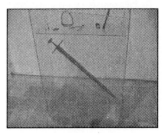

Later that day we turned up at the country retreat of our host and met his charming father. The old expressions *"like father - like son"* and *"Handsome is as handsome does"* could not be more true of theses two. Vaclav's Dad was also a widely travelled geologist, artist and thinker. They were smiling and gardening and pottering around as we pulled up. The temperature dropped overnight but the warmth of the welcome more than compensated.

The Sloup day – the reason for the trip.
Up and away for the run to Sloup (pronounced slope with a slight 'schl' as in schloss at the beginning) in the Ceska Lipa region to the north of Prague. From the car park you look up at the sheer walls created from the remains of a volcanic plug. Montsegur.. Sion..? Clambering up the narrow stone steps and wooden stairs the feeling of pilgrimage and effort is evinced in every step. Vaclav kindly paid the man and left a copy of Sylvia Beamon's book – *"The Royston Cave – Used by Saints or Sinners?"* while we went in search of the cave that allegedly matched

Royston in Hertfordshire. We made our way through the chambers carved from the very rock, past the strange carved lion and panther which stood guard either side of an opening, sentinels to the light that fed into the heart of the monastic rooms of the hermitage. Just to the right of the rock window and contemporary to the sentinels, a portrayal of a portcullis style cage door. Was the mason/artist carving a reference to the Coliseum or some other place that awesome animals were used to strike fear into the early Christians hearts or were they commemorating an earlier pilgrim's visit to the zoos of the Caliphates.

As we arrived at the barred door to the bell shaped chamber that contained the wonderful carvings of the Templars *maybe* the gatekeeper arrived with the keys to allow our entry. Vaclav had spoken Czech words of explanation about our visit and with our wives we were shown into the 'cave' and given the keys to allow us personal and uninterrupted study time in the chamber. I was very privileged and such an accommodation may not be always available.

My eyes focussed on a number of 'wheels' or naïve stars in circles. At least two crucifixion scenes were visible carved into the sandstone and there were a sea of small faces – possibly depictions of skulls. I also noticed a small niche cut at low level blackened across its base by candle wax. There were small faces and tiny faces and then larger faces. Hearts with crosses in them. Small figures of people about 75 – 100mm carrying poles or pikestaffs or possibly a banner were also to be found. The Templar cross patée in a circle was visible - or was it purely a geometrical depiction of a star carved with a compass? Whatever these carvings represented there was a lot of the decoration to be considered.

The accepted wisdom is that the opening of today, with the gateway into the chamber, was a later addition. The light down into the bell chamber would have been from the 500mm wide access shaft above. People or objects must have been let down into the chamber. This indicated several things. This would have been a place of unutterable darkness if the access hole were capped. The pitch black would only be broken by unbearable daylight or moonlight when the hole was opened up. Was this a place of absolute contemplation? The ultimate hermitage with only a glimmer of the saints around you. It was big enough for four adults to walk about in an upright position with space and a little comfort. So, as an oubliette* it would have been bigger than it need be. Not spacious or comfortable but possibly bigger than it needed to be. As the rock had a history of sacred use this seemed an unlikely place for such a place of punishment. In the context of the semi darkness of the hole this seems to be more like an aid to contemplation or in total darkness even a form of early Christian Braille – a sensory aid to remembering ancient forbears and saints who had carried the burden of belief before, found by touch in small light.

On leaving the cave we made our way around the continuation of the rock pathway hewn from the exterior of the uppermost part of the mountain. There was a gentle ascent and a semi circular wind around the top of the outcrop leading up to the hole, which had previously been the entry to the cave. On the left a dramatic sheer drop to the valley floor below and on the right of the pathway a number of arched panels cut from the rock which tradition suggested were used to contain iconographic details. That the whole had some ritualistic and sacred use was, for me, quite apparent.

As we descended the stone steps, I recall, my excited speculations included:

1. The cave was a place of interment for religious artefacts or even an ossuary – it would be difficult to dig graves in solid rock and if you were going to place the respected bones with reverence into the ground where better to place them – in a decorated shrine with the faces of the forbears watching over the bodies forever.
2. Was this a cave made to celebrate Royston? That depends on the ancientness of Royston. The alternative was also a real possibility, - was Royston was carved to commemorate

or recreate Sloup?

3. Here was a cave cut to facilitate the celebration of something akin to the Masonic Royal Arch ceremony in which the main protagonists are let down into the vaults under the Temple in Jerusalem to discover the histories and secrets of the earlier Temples built on the same site.

4. Someone artistic and Christian was thrown down a hole by a pagan and decided to carve his/her ceremonial crosses into the chamber to while away the hours and enhance their devotions.

5. The cave was carved as a cell for the contemplation of death and rebirth. There was a definite spiral like progression up to the top of the rocky mass from a lower level (where there was a ritual bath for the cleansing of the priests or monks) up to the higher level with the hole in the rock leading down into the bell chamber. The path was enriched with the panels or niches (now devoid of iconographic material) leading up or down the path. Where better to enter darkness before being reborn into the light? Reincarnation, resurrection or ritual rebirth in any religion amounts to the same thing. Darkness followed by light - night being reborn into day - each day.

6. The chamber was a place of ritual contemplation before achieving knighthood – those seeking the exaltation of knighthood had to undertake periods of privation and silent contemplation, in complete isolation. Black into white like the Beauseant - again symbolic of a ritual rebirth.

One thing seemed strange – if the later horizontal entry door was indeed cut later why did the carvings seem to stop either side of the door with un-carved space to spare? If the carvings were part of the adornment process for an ossuary or a contemplation aid in the bell shaped cave, why stop carving at all around your circular form. The greater glorification of your god would demand that you adorned your space as much as possible. There was no time restriction on completion in any of the circumstances I had considered. So why stop the carving process? The light from the entry point must have given relief to the carvings on the opposite chamber face. It did not need to be carved all round as the viewer was looking into the chamber.

Of these ideas, looking back my favoured guess and intuition said '2'. Sloup was in easy striking distance of other Czech-land Templar holdings. Kutna Hora had silver mines and the Cistercian monastery, and, strangely, a more recent heritage of old ossuaries and skulls. Czesky Dhub had a Johannite preceptory and Mladislav Boreslav had the valley side castle, the 'Templ', the caves and the above all "The" Norman sword. Cjeskovice to the South, also had a Templar heritage now helping to consolidate the character of the regions wine producing in the excellent Templarski wines. If the brethren had seen and understood the cave at Sloup in their travels through central Europe, and were looking for a place to recreate their sacred find the underground chamber at Royston provided the perfect opportunity.

The fact that both caves are carved in a stone that is a reasonably worked medium is not sufficient, in itself, to tell us that they were worked at or near the same time. There are however, many similarities, to my mind, so numerous to suggest a common tradition and time of production. Stars, wheels, or centred circles, Catherine wheels - perhaps. Sadly, none were as clearly connected as the star and Saint in Royston. Many other connectors exist. Ladders, gridirons or griddles. Hearts and hands with crosses incised. Grouped crucifixion scenes not exceeding 200 mm in width of height. There are a number of individual carvings of unknown people or saints. Their tunic clad bodies above triangular shaped 'skirts' or aprons with hands on hips in a consistent style with a pose like teapot handles. The hair or headgear emphasised like stereotyped pigtails.

Just below these figures in Sloup is, for me, the single most important connection between Sloup and Royston. The Palestinian axe features in both sets of carvings. The axe looks like a child's drawing of an upturned boat without a sail – a half moon shape with a stick as shown in fig X. Why is it important and a connection –well because a similar shaped symbol may be found in the graffiti associated with the Templars in the tower of Chinon* where they were held from 1307. The symbol resembles the 'Cretan' double headed axe – a symbol of double power: Temporal and spiritual; it puts to death and brings back to life! (This place had been a place of ritual and contemplation - others will say for how long. I will just savour my thoughts and encourage others to go and feel their way to their own answers...

(*Chinon was the home of the French philosopher, satirist and wit, Rabelais who coined the phrase *"Eat like a Templar, Drink like a Templar"* in his work, 'Pantagruel'. He also coined the phrase *"Do as thou wilt"* and wrote on 'Thelema' four centuries before a certain Alistair Crowley – funny how the Templars link with the occult so often!)

Templars and Cistercians in England
By Evelyn Lord

Introduction

The Knights Templar and the Cistercians arrived in England at about the same time, c1128-1129. Although the two orders came from different backgrounds, they intersected under the guidance of St Bernard of Clairvaux. His vision turned the Cistercians into one of the great monastic orders of the medieval period, and the Knights Templar into the New Knighthoood of Christ.

Around 1098 a group of monks at the Burgundian Benedictine monastery of Molesme sought to return to the original aims of St Benedict; that is a life of prayer and the worship of God in a desert place, stripped of what they saw in their monastery as the accretions of luxury. In search of spiritual fulfilment they left Molesme to find their 'desert' at Citeaux. At this point they did not wish to break with the Benedictines but wanted to observe the Benedictine Rule in its purity, and to impose a uniformity on the governance of the monasteries. Uniformity was to be maintained through an annual general chapter meeting, and an annual visitation of all Cistercian abbeys. The first annual general chapter meeting was held under the auspices of the English abbot of Citeaux, Stephen Harding who had succeeded the first Cistercian abbot Robert in 1109. This chapter was the first sign that the Cistercians although seeking to abide by the Benedictine Rule were in fact treading a different path. It was Stephen who introduced ideas about worshipping in simplicity; in unadorned churches stripped of ornament. He set the Cistercians on the road to austerity, but it was an energetic and articulate young Burgundian nobleman Bernard, who became the abbot of Clairvaux who gave the Cistercians their identity as a separate order, and drew up the strict guidelines by which they were to live, far from the concourse of men.

The Knights Templar, of course, were founded by a different route and initially had different aims. They did not wish to live far from the concourse of men, but to engage in concourse for a specific purpose – the protection of pilgrims to the Holy Land, and ultimately the maintenance of the Christian presence there. In c1109 Hugh de Payens, another Burgundian, and a group of nine fellow knights were given quarters in the Temple of Solomon, and so became the Knights of the Temple. They vowed that when not on duty as soldiers for Christ, they would live a monastic life of poverty, chastity and obedience.

In 1127 Hugh and five other knights came west to gain recognition for their order. Hugh put his case forward at the Council of Troyes, and he was given support by his fellow Burgundian, Bernard of Clairvaux. Hugh and Bernard came from the same social background, and it is possible that they were already acquainted before the Council of Troyes. It was Bernard who drew up the Templar Rule for Hugh. There were many similarities between this and the Cistercian statutes, and the organisation of the Templar order bore many similarities to that of the Cistercians. An annual general chapter meeting for example, and the appointment of visitors who travelled round each province on a tour of inspection are directly related to the Cistercian organisation. In England the annual general chapter meeting was held in different preceptories, although Temple Dinsley in Hertfordshire was the favourite location. We know that the province of England was under visitation in 1307 as Himbert Blank, the visitor was arrested and tried in England.

In the Rule allowances had to be made for when the Templars were out of the cloister and on military campaign. Bernard saw the Templars as an instrument for returning the Holy Land to Christian control, and with this in mind he persuaded the pope to launch the second crusade. He justified the Templars, a religious order, in shedding blood in *De Laudae Novae Militae* (In

Praise of the New Knighthood), writing that there was no sin in killing the enemies of God. Were the Templars the military wing of the Cistercians? J.T. Fowler claimed that this was so, and that in all the Cistercians included seven orders of knights in their organisation. There is no actual evidence for this statement, but it is clear that Bernard was closely involved with the Templars.

Both the Cistercians and the Templars needed an income, and in the Middle Ages income came from land. Extension of their lands was essential for the Cistercians, as when a monastery reached a certain size it had to send out a colony of monks to found another house. Citeaux, the oldest of the Cistercian abbeys founded four daughter houses, and all Cisterican houses could trace their origins back to one of these, for example the Cistercian abbey of Boxley in Kent was in the Clairvaux lineage.

The foundation of Templar preceptories was more random and occurred where ever the Templars were granted land, but as both the Cistercians and Templars were late comers to landed society in England they were often given marginal land which needed clearing or draining before it could become productive.

Land Management

The Cistercians had clear aims laid out for them in their statutes on how they should manage their estates. Direct cultivation of the land by lay brothers was to be preferred to leasing it out. Their ideal was not to conform to the communal open field agriculture of medieval Europe but to build up blocs of land that they farmed separately by themselves. Their characteristic way of doing this was by founding granges. Granges were large farmsteads, with a barn or *grangia*, a hall and dormitory for the brothers, sheepfolds, cattle pens and depending on the area a defensive wall, bank or ditch. The grange was ' the most important single contribution of the new monastic orders and particularly the Cistercians to the landscape and economy of the 12th and 13th centuries.'

Excavations at Templar preceptories in England show that a similar layout to that of the grange was used. At South Witham in Lincolnshire, for example, there was a fully developed farmyard with barns and storerooms, a hall, dormitory and chapel, group around a courtyard and enclosed within a wall. At Strood in Kent there was a large complex of buildings including a hall, chamber, buttery, kitchen and chapel, and a five bay barn, whilst the barns at Cressing Temple in Essex are surviving evidence of the Templars' work.

Work on the Templars land was either done servile tenants or hired help, and in this they differ from the Cistercians who preferred to use lay brothers attached to the order. The early Cistercian statutes forbade the ownership of serfs, but because of the economics of production this statute was soon broken.

Some Templar sergeants worked and managed Templar estates, but the Templars' also employed bailiffs who were paid through rent free grants of land. The Templars' aim in farming their estates was to make a maximum profit, a percentage of which could be sent east. However, some donors of land to the Templars stated that all profits must go east, for example as in the grant of Rothley in Leicstershire by John Harcourt. The aim of Templars in making their land profitable was not dissimilar to Cistercian aims. The Cistercian Chapter General organised collections from all Cistercian abbeys. Each abbey was assessed and provincial abbots collected the money and sent it to the general chapter.

Although both the Templars and the Cistercians wanted to make a maximum profit from their estates in England there is no evidence that they farmed these differently to other lay or ecclesiastical landlords of the time. Evidence from Hertfordshire for example shows that other ecclesiastical landlords, such as the Abbey of St Albans were harsher landlords than the Templars, exacting rigorous labour service and fines from their tenants.

Evidence for actual profits from Templar land in England is

scarce, but we do know that like the Cistercians they made the best of what they were given, and their husbandry reflected the geographical conditions of each preceptory, for example barley was grown at Weston in Hertfordshire, which remained a prime barley growing area into the nineteenth century. In the Cotswold and on the Wiltshire downs the Templars maintained sheep walks with flocks of up to 1000 sheep. The existence of fulling mills on Templars' property suggests that they were manufacturing cloth, whilst the barley at Weston was turned into malt for brewing. In Temple Ewell in Kent there were 49 sheepfolds, pigs and oxen were kept, and part of the tenants' labour service was to bring herrings back from market.

The Cistercian exploited their holdings in a similar way, with sheep walks where appropriate, fishing on the coast, and iron working and a textile industry on the Kentish Weald.

Conclusion

This short paper indicates that the organisation of the Knights Templar in England bore a resemblance to that of the Cistercian, and that this goes back to the influence of St Bernard of Clairvaux who drew up the Templar Rule. Whether St Bernard thought that the Knights Templar were a military branch of the Cistercians we shall never know. At a local level in England the Templars and the Cistercians organised their estates in a similar way, and with the same ultimate aim, the glory of God; the Cistercians through contemplation and the Templars through action.

Did the Templars survive in Scotland?
By Hugh Montgomery

There have been countless stories written about the supposed survival of the Templars in Scotland. It has been stated that they were the troops who charged to the rescue of the Scots at the battle of Bannockburn. It has been believed that there are certain Sinclair Charters which show that they continued after the arrest of their Grand Master and the subsequent witch- hunt by the French king and the Papacy.

The purpose of this article is to look at what documentary evidence there is and to try to come to some sort of logical conclusion. Let me start by stating quite categorically that I do not and have never accepted the theory of the Priory of Sion as some sort of hidden secret society behind the Order of the Temple.

Let us look first at Bannockburn. This was first brought to the attention of the general public by Messers. Baigent, Leigh & Lincoln in their book *The Holy Blood and The Holy Grail*[1]. They state 'a sizeable contingent is said to have fought at Robert the Bruce's side at the Battle of Bannockburn', but they give no reference. This therefore must be said to be *unproven*.

Next let us look at the Larmenius Charter. According to this Jacques de Molay left instructions on his death for a certain Palestinian born Christian called John Mark Larmenius to succeed him. A copy of this Charter is in the possession of Mark Mason's Hall in London. Whether this charter is valid or not I cannot say but I understand that recent research and tests suggest that it may be older than first thought. The interesting thing about this Charter is that it contains the words 'I, lastly…will say and order that the Scot-Templars deserters of the Order, be blasted by an anathema'.

If this charter is genuine then there were Templars in Scotland who had deserted the Order. But how or why did they desert? Perhaps by giving up their vows of Chastity?

Perhaps by returning to live with their families?

There is however an even more interesting document and that is a Safe Conduct issued by the English dated 24th October 1358 for some 60 mounted 'Knights and Men-at-Arms of the Temple to 'Go abroad''[2]. There were three groups of some 60 each. The first was led Alexander de Montgomery, the younger son of Alexander de Montgomerie and a second group was led by a Sinclair[3]. They were going to join their brothers of the Sword in Livonia. In fact we know that most perished in a bog in Livonia. Two survived to tell the tale. What is interesting here is that the group is specifically referred to as 'of the Temple'. Now that seems to me to show beyond reasonable doubt that they were regarded as Templars. The other interesting point is that they went to join their 'brothers of the sword'. The Order of the Sword or to give it its correct name The Brotherhood of the Sword had been formed at least under the auspices of the Knights Templar if not as a daughter Order, in much the same way as the Teutonic Knights. The task of the Brotherhood of the Sword was to forge out a new land in Livonia. In the event they were unsuccessful.

One thing is clear. We have a group of unmarried (possibly celibate) Scots Knights and Men-at-Arms, who are members of a Temple and who are going to join a group which was formed from or by the old Templar Order.

What intrigues me however is why should they have survived in Scotland and not anywhere else? The only place in which the Templars survived intact and unchanged was Spain, where the king of Spain simply took the Templars based there under his protection and changed their name to 'The Knights of Christ' and made them a Spanish Order.

So was there a reason for the Templars to survive in Scotland? The clue lies in the names of the leaders of these groups, who went to Livonia – Sinclair and Montgomery. For those of you who have read my book 'The God-Kings of Europe', you will know that these families were amongst the most important branches of the Ulvungar dynasty and I have developed this further in my new book 'The God-Kings of England' published by The Temple Publications. But what you may ask has the Knights Templar and the Ulvungars in common?

The Knights Templar bear all the hallmarks of a much older warrior group, The Joms-Vikings of Scandinavia. This was a religious group dedicated to Odin, who lived a life in barracks without marriage, though probably not without women. They were devoted to the cult of Odin and their highest ideal was to die in battle and thereby be reunited in Valhalla with their God. Only those warriors of proven worth and valour were eligible to join. One of their commanders, Sven Forkbeard, when he became King of England formed his own Joms-Viking band, called the Housecarls. It was they, as the personal guard of King Harold, himself descended via his mother from Sven Forkbeard, who took such a toll on their cousins, the Normans, at Hastings [4].

The founder of the Templars and their first Grand Master was called Hughes de Payen (1070-1131) and was descended from a certain Tiraud de Payen (1012-1063) who was called curiously 'The Moor of Gardille'. Now de Payen actually does not make much sense but the Latinised version of his name *Paganos* does. It means pagan. So Hughes de Payan was actually Hugh the Pagan. This suggests that the family was not originally Christian but pagan, and generally the Church by pagan meant 'The Vikings'. However if his grandfather was called The Moor, this suggests that the family was not Caucasian, but very dark maybe even black originally. If you look carefully at my genealogies in the God-Kings of Europe it is noticeable that there are many with dark skin, particularly those descended from Mary Magdalene and who married back into the Ulvungar dynasty[5]. Was therefore Hughes de Payen actually a member of the Ulvungar dynasty?

The answer I am afraid is that I do not know, but there is a Scottish Family of MacGregor-Pagan who are, what is more his liege lord the Count of Champagne most certainly was 6. What is interesting is that almost all of the original Knights Templar had been married before becoming Templars, including, as will be seen from the genealogy below, Hughes de Payen. What is more he and his wife had a family. So what happened to this family de Payen? Where did they go? I would suggest that some stayed in France in Champagne but that one branch at least finished up in Scotland. I have not yet had the chance of investigating all of the genealogies of the so-called founders of the Templars, but it would not surprise me to learn that most, if not all, were descended from one branch or another of the Ulvungars.

It should be noted that one of their earliest Grand Commanders was called Odon (1156) and that the Knights Templar were forbidden to accept ransom and if necessary had to fight to the death. Shades of the Joms-Vikings!

Did they survive in Scotland? If, as I suspect, the Knights Templar were originally a form of House carls for the Kings of Jerusalem, who were themselves Ulvungars, then 'Yes' they would have been protected by other Ulvungar families and some of the most influential were in Scotland.

I have written this short article in the hope that some of your readers will contribute more information about the genealogies concerned, so that together we can plot the probable interconnections between the various families of the founders.

Tibaud de Payen 6
(The Moor of Gadille)
(1012-1063)

Tibaud de Payen
(1035-1094)

Adelaide de Payen = Hugues de Chaumont
(1036-1098)   (Lord of Gisors)
(1032-1075)

Hugues de Payen = Catherine de Chaumont
(1070-1131)

They had issue

Did the Templars survive in Scotland? An update
By Hugh Montgomery

In a previous Temple booklet I wrote an article about the family of Hugh de Payen and the survival of the Knights Templars. The article was written in good faith on the basis of the information I then had. As it turns out that information was almost totally erroneous. About six months ago I was able to access certain documents which paint a very different picture.

Hugh de Payen as founder of the Knights Templar is only mentioned by William of Tyre in *Rerum in Partibus Transmarinis Gestarum,* which was written in about 1200 AD or about eighty years after the founding of the Order. In the German version *Die lateinische Fortsetzung XII, 7, pp. 520-521* we learn that he was a knight from Champagne. In the original Latin version he is called Pagano and Odericus Vitalis writing in Latin also calls him Pagano or Paganis. It is only in a late and very poor Medieval French translation, which became very popular in the Middle Ages, that he becomes Hughes de Payen. Sir Steven Runciman in his History of the Crusades used the German and French versions and called him Hughes de Payen and scholars who have followed Sir Steven have followed suit. I do not think however that Sir Steven was particularly interested in Hughes ancestors. He was after all writing a History of an event not a genealogical study.

It has since become clear that Hughes real name was Hugh fitzPayen or FitzPagan and that his true genealogy is as given below. Full details can be found in Appendix U of my book *The God-Kings of Outremer:*

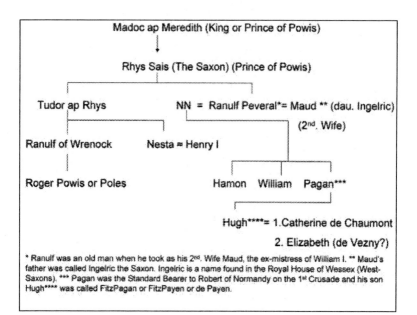

* Ranulf was an old man when he took as his 2nd. Wife Maud, the ex-mistress of William I. ** Maud's father was called Ingelric the Saxon. Ingelric is a name found in the Royal House of Wessex (West-Saxons). *** Pagan was the Standard Bearer to Robert of Normandy on the 1st Crusade and his son Hugh**** was called FitzPagan or FitzPayen or de Payen.

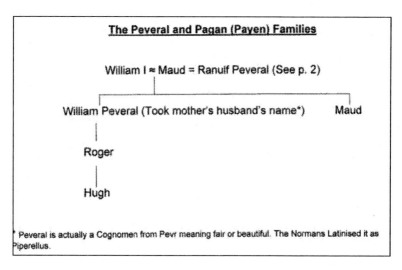

The Peveral and Pagan (Payen) Families

* Peveral is actually a Cognomen from Pevr meaning fair or beautiful. The Normans Latinised it as Piperellus.

The Origins of Head Worship
By Oddvar Olsen

Are people still worshipping decapitated heads? Did they ever? In this article we shall delve into the deep recesses of human consciousness and explore the possibility of head worshipping cults and examine if they did and for what reason? The first time I heard about legends connected with head worship was when I read about the Knights Templar who dug up (in what sounds like complete madness), the head of his beloved, the Lady of Maraclea. The story relates:

> "A great lady of Maraclea was loved by a Templar, a Lord of Sidon; but she died in her youth, and on the night of her burial, this wicked lover crept to the grave, dug up her body and violated it. Then a voice from the void bade him return in nine months time for he would find a son. He obeyed the injunction and at the appointed time he opened the grave again and found a head on the leg bones of the skeleton (skull and crossbones). The same voice bade him 'guard it well, for it would be the giver of all good things', and so he carried it away with him. It became his protecting genius, and he was able to defeat his enemies by merely showing them the magic head. In due course, it passed into the possession of the Order. [1]

Rather morbid! Was this but an invention I wondered; a 'spin' of the medieval writers to further blackened the already tainted reputation of the Knights Templar? Or did the story/legend have any foundation in earlier traditions?

Many secret societies have been seen as sinister, which is not a big surprise, at least for the person that sees the Knights Templar as such a society and also the alleged forerunners of numerous secret societies and also Freemasonry. The latter fraternity claim their use of skulls but as a symbol of mortality like when the candidate is raised in the 3rd degree. Couldn't they as readily have used a foot, maybe a hand?

Another shadowy society is the *Skull and Crossbones*, which originated at Yale University, USA in 1832. The *Bonesmen* society includes many prominent figures such as the Bush Presidents, in which case, I can believe that the skull is a symbol of death and mortality, certainly this is much more plausible than as a symbol of the intellect and something positive!

In John Stubbs' recent book *DONNE: The Reformed Soul* he tells us that the splendid John Donne (1572-1631) inherited Sir Thomas More's (1478-1535) skull. Although they were related, I found this a very curious thing to have happened, even though Donne was one of the most prominent metaphysical poets of his age. For a month More's body was placed over London Bridge before his daughter rescued it. Some legends claims it was thrown in to the Thames; others that it resides in the Roper Vault of St. Dunstan's, Canterbury and others that More's body was buried at the Tower of London, in the chapel of St. Peter and Vincula.

A great number of painters have also depicted contemplation of a skull such as in the *Portrait of Katheryn of Berain* by Adrian van Cronenburgh, Frans Hals', *Youth with a Skull* and in paintings of Mary Magdelene by artists like El Greco and Gustave Dore. And of course there is the much discussed bas relief on the altar of Mary Magdelene in Rennes-le-Château. Even the great Shakespear in *Hamlet*, Act 5 Scene 1 has Yoric skull exhumed. So what does this all allude to?

The fact is that heads and skulls have been much revered on every continent from the earliest times. Without detailing its importance in Tibet, in African and South American tribal communities, we shall primarily discuss their importance in what became the Western mystery tradition.

The western mystery tradition stems from various traditions from the Middle East, Norse and Celtic mythology. Adam, who is God's first human creation according to Christians, Jews and Muslims, also had his head cut off after his death. Religious texts have it that his head is buried at Golgotha, *the place of the Skull*. Some historians claim at Hebron, but where, doesn't concern this study. What is important is that his head was buried to protect the land and its residents. The father of the British Isles, Bran the Blessed's head was buried at Tower Hill for the same reasons as Adam's and also to secure the surrounding land with protection and fertility.

In the Greek legends, we learn that both Medusa and Orpheus are decapitated. When the latter's head is found, it will sing and foretell the future. Osiris, after being mutilated by his jealous brother Set was thrown into the Nile where Isis finds him lodged in a tamarisk bush that has turned into a mighty tree (which symbolises creation). Norse mythology tells us that Odin preserved the head of the wisest of gods Mimir in herbs to obtain knowledge from it. St John the Baptist, suffering decapitation at the request of the alluring Salome, is perhaps one of the most talked about story. This strange request by Salome has spurned many popular authors who claim that the Knights Templar came into possession of the Baptist's head. Keith Laidler in his *'The Head of God'* is perhaps the most prominent promulgator of this thesis. Laidler not only claims that the Templars were in possession of John the Baptist's head, but also that they possessed the head of Jesus. He continues that the Templars were inheritors of an ancient mystery cult of the head.

These theories have rejuvenated the 'worship of the severed head' phenomena. It seems fascinating. It is weird, even though macabre for it is juicy and has become a focus point of many Templar buffs.

Instead of rehashing the old story of Templar head worship, where Baphomet has so often been discussed, we shall instead bring the story into a new perspective. However, it needs to be briefly mentioned that the Templar knights were accused of worshipping a head. The eminent historian Dr Helen Nicholson in *The Knights Templar - A New History* tells us that the Order possessed the *head* of St Euphemia in the church at Nicosia in Cyprus. Dr Nicholson continues that this was probably where the *head* accusations against the Templars originated. Another more discussed head is the one found in the Paris Preceptory, Caput 58 or Head 58. During the trials Brother William of Arreblay, (former almoner to King Philip IV of France) informs the Inquisition that he believed this to be the head of one of the 11,000 virgins martyred with St Ursula at Cologne at the beginning of the fourth century. Suffice it to say that the few brothers that had seen this *head* described it in many grotesque guises, with several faces, of cats and in different colours.

The much-debated Templecombe wall painting shown below is dated to the Templar era and was found close to their Preceptory there has fused speculations of the Knights Templar as *head worshippers*.

In 2006, I was advised on a wooden head at St James' Church, Cameley. Cameley is a tiny village, 1.5 miles from Templecloud and 11 miles south of St Cross' Templar church at Bristol. We know that Cameley belonged to the Templar order as it is confirmed by a Charter of 1201 that King John granted holdings there to the Templars. At the time of writing we are awaiting a carbon dating of this head.

During the trails of the Templars it is said that their last grand Master, William de la More had secreted four of the Templars items/idols from France. I must remind the reader that some of the later authors say it was four heads, but this it is not so; the court papers states four icons or idols. But two heads in two Templar locations! Could there possibly been any more?

Having for numerous years been researching the Templars in Somerset I was now prompted to look for other heads. And by finally realising the most obvious, which is that nearly all Templar holdings lie next to the old Roman roads and Pilgrim routes, I was to discover more heads. Although, I am not at present able to prove that they have any connections with the Templar brethren, a couple are worth including as examples. These heads were found in churches dating from the 1100's to 1300's.

Four Heads at St Andrews Church, Blagdon

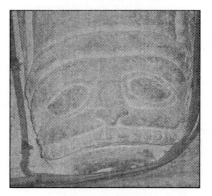

The three photos above have a certain flavour of the 'green man' found in the Templar Preceptory at Garway. (below). Similar 'cat's heads' may be seen in Temple Bruer, Lincolnshire and Temple Church, London. Compton Martin and Blagdon are only a few miles west of Cameley, close to West Harptree where the Templars held a vast estate just off the Roman road leading to Uphill, which is suggested being a Templar port.

The Celts are the most documented European heritage that we know associated decapitated heads with special powers. The Roman historian Livy (59 B.C. – 17 A.D.) described how Celtic warriors decorated skulls with gold and used them as cups for offerings to the gods. Drinking chalices made of skulls have also been recorded in the Norse legends. The Celts are known to have had the heads of their enemies dangling from belts around their waist. In my opinion this is a more basic way to show the strength of the warrior, although in the case of using a skull as a drinking vessel, I propose that they thought they would gain the power of the victim.

Another tradition that of worshipping heads near Holy Wells have been carrying on as the Catholic Church let the lay people still make their offerings in such places until quite recently. To mention a few examples; a known skull and well cult existed at Llandeilo Llwydairth, at Odell in Bedfordshire a skull has been discovered inserted in the lining at a Roman well and decapitations near wells in France are recorded by Gregory of Tours in the sixth century.

Yuri Leitch pointed out the interesting similarity between the decapitation of St Clair and his relative St Nectarn in issue number 9 of *The Temple*. As we know, a host of other authors claim strong links with the St Clair's Rosslyn Chapel and the Knights Templar. To recount briefly:

"I discussed the most likely origin of the name 'Sinclair' to a 6th century Cornish saint (St. Cleer) and told of his tragic death, being decapitated by two knights, and how, miraculously, the headless body of St. Cleer carried his own head to a sacred well, before dying.) Imagine my surprise then, when I learnt that St. Nectan was St. Cleer's older brother! Both sons of the famous King Brychan of Wales. Stranger still is that both brothers died in almost identical ways. St. Cleer was beheaded by two knights and St. Nectan was beheaded by two robbers. Both brothers pick up their decapitated heads and each carries it to a sacred well."[2]

What we cannot argue against but must admit, as fact is all the Holy Wells have been attributed to healing and fertility. Are the legends of St Clair of St Nectarn metaphors of the same? Were their heads put in wells for healing, fertility and protection of the surrounding landscape like as with Adam and Bran?

The Green Man has also to be taken into account. This evergreen head (like the ever flowing water in wells) with foliage sprouting from his mouth (sometimes ears and nose too) is a symbol of regeneration and rebirth. His emanating foliage may also symbolise the creation, by the Logo, the word; ever creating and evolving. The importance of the Green Man is easily appreciated due to the abundance of depictions found of this ancient symbol. Originally a Pagan deity, he can be found throughout the Middle East and in churches in Europe. Like the decapitated head; as symbol of protection, of knowledge, healing, fertility and rebirth, the Green Man serves his role well in this account.

We must now return briefly to Cameley and it must be mentioned that as with the Templecombe head the Cameley head has been hidden away at times. However, at the time of writing it may viewed in the twelfth century St James' Church. I must draw attention to the striking coat of arms of Charles I also located in Cameley church. Originally it decorated most of the south wall (where the head is too); today sadly only fragments are visible. As

I am sure you agree, this is a most *potent* Unicorn adorning this Coat of Arms. As we know Charles I was beheaded... but do not let us fall into the trap of too much speculation.

To conclude, we have through this short article learnt that attributes of Holy wells, the Green Man, the phallus and decapitated heads are symbolising pretty much the same, if not all the same. Symbols, of protection, regeneration, precognition, wisdom, fertility and creation. The Skull/Head cult has now come to light as nothing terribly sinister, dark or disturbing but as a symbol of well being, of healing, of continuations, of life in a complete and positive state of evolution.

Chapter 3 References:

The Templar Beauceant

1   Upton-Ward. J.M *The Rule of the Templars, p 11,* Boydell Press, Woodbridge, 2002
2   Addison C. G. *The History of Knights Templar, p 40* Adventure Unlimited Press, Illinois, 2001
3   Ibid p50
4   Ibid p161
5   Macoy R. *History of Knights Templars, p 108,* Masonic Publishing Company, New York 1874
6   Ibid p123
7   Ibid

The Cameley Head – An Enigma

1   *The Trail of the Templars.* M Barber, 1978
2   http://www.crystalinks.com
3   http://www.crystalinks.com
4   *In search of the Knights Templar,* Simon Brighton, 2006
5   *Les Secret de la Chevalerie* Victor Emile Michelet, 1930

Did the Templars survive in Scotland?

1   Baigent, Leigh & Lincoln (1982) – *The Holy Blood & The Holy Grail,* p.78 Corgi edition
2   The Order of the Fleur-de-Lys (2006) -*The History of the Order of the Fleur-de-Lys.* www.order-of-the-fleur-de-lys.org; Also Montgomery, H. (2002) – The Montgomery Millennium, p. 7, Megatrend
3   Sinclair Charter Chest courtesy of Niven Sinclair
4   Seward, D. (1973) – *The Monks of War,* Arkana
4   Montgomery, H. (2006) – *The God-Kings of Europe,* p.154, The Book Tree
5   Montgomery, H. (2007) – *The God-Kings of England,* The Temple Publications.

6   Chaumont Family archives quoted by Baigent et al *op. cit.* p.442

The Origins of Head Worship

1   Ward J. S. M., *Freemasonry and the Ancient Gods.* Kessinger Publishing Co. 1996
2   Olsen. O. Ed., *The Templar Papers*, New Page Books, 2006

Sources:

Broadhurst P, *The Green Man and the Dragon*, Mythos Press, 2006
Frye R M, *Ladies, Gentlemen, and Skulls: Hamlet and the Iconographic Traditions, Shakespeare Quarterly, Vol. 30, No. 1*
Laidler K, *The Head of God*, Weidenfield and Nicholson, 1998
Nicholson Dr H, *The Knights Templar - A New History.* Sutton, 2001
Olsen. O. Ed., *The Templar Papers*, New Page Books, 2006
Shakespeare W, *The Complete Works*, Ed. Alexander P, Collins, 1954
Stubbs J, *DONNE: The Reformed Soul.* Penguin Books. 2007

Chapter 4

Shakespeare and Hermetic Magic
By Atasha Fyfe

The traditional academic approach to Shakespeare's plays is to examine them in isolation, as stand-alone works of literature. But their historical context provides many keys and clues which throw fresh light on both the plays and their author. During that time, Hermeticism was one of the most important mainsprings of change. It had an enormous influence on the religious reformations and creative flowering now called The Renaissance. Like a stone thrown into a pond, Hermetic thinking rippled out, creating far-reaching political and social changes as well. There is much to suggest that Shakespeare and his theatre company were more deeply involved with these undercurrents than is usually supposed.

Hermetic philosophy was introduced to Western Europe by Cosimo de Medici, when in 1460 he acquired from the black market the complete Greek text of the Corpus Hermeticum. This was a collection of about forty books of teachings, philosophy and magical practices all apparently written by the ancient Egyptian god Thoth. In Greek, Thoth translated into Hermes and came to be called Hermes Trismegistus – Thrice-Great Hermes. It's now thought that the Hermetica were written in or near Alexandria sometime between 200BC and 200AD. Although several writers contributed to the Corpus, they all asserted that Thoth was in one way or another their source or inspiration. When the Library of Alexandria burned down, the Hermetica somehow escaped. During the subsequent dark ages it underwent a curious 1500 years journey. Kept hidden most of the time, it was constantly one step ahead of persecution, war or fire.

When Cosimo de Medici finally held the Corpus in his hands, he realised it would be the prize in his collection of ancient philosophies. But he was getting old, and didn't understand Greek. Accordingly, he instructed Ficino to translate it as quickly as possible, so that he could read it before he died. The translated version was later published in 1471. Already steeped in Platonic philosophy, the Florentine academy embraced the Hermetica with enthusiasm, and its influence spread rapidly from there.

An important carrier of these new ideas to England was Anne Boleyn - mother of the future Queen Elizabeth I. She came from Provence, where, despite Papal opposition, courtly life was full of Gnostic philosophies of love and alchemy. These ideals were spread by the Troubadours throughout Europe. The rose became their symbol of courtly love, and heretical thinking was the soil from which it grew. When Anne came to the English court and later married Henry VIII, she brought those influences to the highest levels of English society. Ironically for Anne, this philosophical ambience may have strengthened Henry's later decision to finalise the break with Rome. By the time of her execution, however, Anne's legacy for the future was established. Her daughter's reign was distinguished by an atmosphere of optimistic freedom in which new ideas and creative thought could flourish in unaccustomed safety.

In earlier centuries, the Knights Templar helped to lay the foundations for these developments. Their white mantles and red cross referred to an alchemical idea. In alchemy, the white rose represented the Princess, or the purified emotions, while the red rose was the Prince, or purified intellect. The symbol of the completion of the Great Work was the unification of the red and white rose. The most famous one was London's New Temple Garden near to the present Inns of Court. This garden was maintained long after the Templars' suppression in 1307, and nearly 150 years later it was here that the houses of Lancaster and

York turned the red and white roses into emblems of war.

When Elizabeth I came to the throne, she was heiress of both those houses, as well as royal inheritor of the Protestant revolution – the newly created Church of England. She took as her emblem the alchemical sign of the combined red and white rose to signify a new era of peace and enlightenment. The Templar thread in this rich tapestry was acknowledged in Edmund Spenser's poem *The Faerie Queen*. Although written in honour of Elizabeth I, its main character and hero was the Red-Cross Knight.

In the courtly world, liberation from Rome began to be celebrated not just in poetry and song, but also with Hermetic masques. These were private amateur dramas, performed mostly by the family and courtiers of the great houses and courts. With fantastical sets, elaborate costumes, and Elizabethan special effects, a story in verse would be enacted. At the end, actors and audience would mingle in a fancy dress ball. On important occasions these could become quite lavish festivals with sometimes two weeks of poetry, music, plays, fireworks, chivalric jousts, exotic costumes and dances. A favourite subject was the connection between the Tudors and King Arthur, identifying the monarch as the source of a revived Arthurian ideal, if not the return of Arthur himself. Despite his distrust of magic, King James enjoyed this theme, and Hermetic masques were as popular at his court as in Elizabethan times.

The masques were also intended to be a kind of magic ritual. Hermetic thinking had given rise to the belief that civilisation was on the brink of a new golden age in which humanity would regain the innate powers and awareness that were lost in 'the fall'. These festivities were specifically designed to create a microcosmic ideal that would mirror and call in the desired macrocosmic reality. By Hermetic magic, the masques would help to create a new golden age.

As a theatrical fashion, masques inevitably influenced the

play-writing of the time. They feature in many of Shakespeare's plays, being directly referred to, or presented as plays-within-plays in *Love's Labours Lost, Romeo and Juliet, Timon of Athens,* and *The Tempest.* Shakespeare would also have been exposed to the Hermetic philosophy behind the masques through his many connections with the courtly world. His personal patron was the Earl of Southampton. His first theatre company, the Lord Chamberlain's Men, was managed by Queen Elizabeth's favoured first cousin. The theatre itself was protected by Robert Dudley, Earl of Leicester – the well-known Queen's favourite. Dudley was also a supporter of John Dee, Elizabeth's chief occult advisor and Hermeticist. James I tightened Shakespeare's connection to the monarch when he brought the best acting companies directly under royal patronage, renaming Shakespeare's group The King's Men. In both reigns they performed at the various royal courts on a regular basis, especially at Christmas, New Year and Shrovetide. These connections alone would have exposed William Shakespeare to the Renaissance ideas that were circulating among the educated and court circles of his time.

Hermetic thinking also spread to the general population. It was in the rougher crucible of the public theatre, through plays by Shakespeare, Marlowe and Jonson, that the new ideas were mirrored, disseminated and critically examined. In *The Elixir and the Stone*, writers Michael Baigent and Richard Leigh say:

"For more than a century after Henry VIII broke with the Church of Rome, no churches were built in England. Instead, England built theatres. Theatre became a new species of church, a new temple. Within this magical structure, the rites and rituals of Hermetic mysteries were performed for an insatiable public".

The theatres being built for these thirsty people were intentionally designed according to Hermetic principles. Older Templar knowledge about the magical effects of architecture surfaced again, contributing to the creation of Elizabethan theatres as a new kind of temple. In the Middle East, Muslim and ancient Judaic taboos on the representation of living things – 'graven images' - had resulted in the development of geometry as the divine blueprint of life. Geometry came to represent sacred immutable principles that underlie and create reality in a god-like way. This found a natural expression in architecture and masonry - especially in the creation of temple-like structures. In their quests to the Holy Land, the Templars absorbed this knowledge and later applied it in the construction of their great Gothic Cathedrals. The concept of magical architecture flowered again when England began to build theatres instead of churches in the 16th century.

The English Hermeticist, Robert Fludd (1574 – 1637), contributed to this theatre building, designing them to be a focus and conduit for higher energies. He also developed special effects, working out how to create the impressions of fire, thunder and cannons on the stage. In Renaissance Europe, Hermetic thinking had inspired great paintings. In Elizabethan England it became inextricably entwined with the dramatic arts.

Perhaps the most famous theatre of that time was The Globe, where most of Shakespeare's plays were performed. Before its construction, the theatre builder James Burbage consulted John Dee. The result was a building designed entirely according to Hermetic principles. The ground plan was based on the four elements within the circle of the zodiac. Propitious astrological angles were built in. A starry awning above the stage represented the cosmos. This theatre was called 'The Globe' because it was meant to serve as a microcosm of the greater reality – 'as above, so below'. Plays performed here were to affect society like a magical talisman, drawing energies from the cosmos through the lens of the play into the world. The concept of the world as a theatre and the theatre as a world (or globe) was often referred to in Shakespeare's plays. The best known of those speeches is

Jacques' "All the world's a stage" in *As You Like It* (2.7)

During the twenty-odd years of Shakespeare's writing career, his plays show a consistent fascination with the occult. A hallmark of Shakespearian drama is the recurring presence of fairies, witches, dreams, visions, prophecies and ghosts. These were more than just flitting phenomena - many of Shakespeare's plays illustrate an in-depth knowledge of occult matters. *Midsummer Night's Dream* is not fully understandable without knowing the complex fairy folk lore upon which the story is based. *Macbeth* reveals a knowledge, and carries an aura, of black magic that is still felt today - especially by theatre people. In *Magick in Theory and Practice*, Aleister Crowley remarked that although the witches' charm in *Macbeth* "was perhaps not meant seriously, its effect is indubitable."

During the course of his career, however, magic in Shakespeare's plays moves from the 'Old Ways' to an almost completely Hermetic outlook. In this, he may have partly reflected and partly led the attitudes of his audience. By the late 16th century, the new Renaissance magic was beginning to show people a way beyond feeling like the constant victims of circumstance through fairy tricks or evil spells. Awareness was growing that it might be possible to use mysterious invisible influences in an enlightened way. Man need no longer be at the whimsical disposal of incomprehensible forces. It might even be possible to understand and use those hidden powers for the betterment of the world, transforming both the individual and society. This sea-change of beliefs about magic can be traced quite clearly in the plays of William Shakespeare.

One of the earliest Shakespearian references to Hermetic ideas is in *Henry IV Pti*, in the magician Glendower, who like John Dee was Welsh. At that time the Welsh were seen as suspicious dabblers in magic. In a somewhat overblown way, Glendower airs a few vaguely Hermetic observations. Hotspur deflates them all with his sharp common sense. When the magician finally declares "I can call spirits from the vasty deep," Hotspur taunts, "But will they come when you do call for them?" And the argument is won, to the probable delight of the audience. By the final plays, however, nearly twenty years later, the magus figure had transformed from the easily ridiculed Glendower into the powerful and learned Prospero. By then Hermetic philosophy had become Shakespeare's overarching theme and subject matter.

A central tenet of Hermeticism is the concept of oneness – that all things are connected in a greater unified whole. This concept of the inter-connectedness of all creation gave rise to a complex system of astrological correspondences between earth and the cosmos. Although Shakespearian characters do refer to this astrological lore, a greater sense of Hermetic oneness is expressed throughout his plays by the unity of tone, characters and action around a central theme. The Shakespearian scholar and critic, G. Wilson-Knight says:

> "Shakespeare seems to subscribe to one of the central principles of occult thought, namely, that man and the world are connected, psyche and matter are connected; the hero and his universe are interdependent."

The legend of the Fisher King illustrates this principle. The king represents the people, and his mysterious wound is theirs, creating the wasteland in which they live. *Hamlet* could be interpreted as a version of that legend, in which the rotten state of Denmark is the wasteland created by his own inner wound. Another possible Hermetic thread in *Hamlet* may be the story of the minor Hermeticist, Tomaso Campanella. While in the prisons of the Inquisition, Tomaso escaped execution by feigning madness. Hamlet adopted the same ruse, while referring to Denmark as 'a prison'. Tomaso was more successful than Hamlet, though. He eventually gained his freedom, and later held secret astrological rituals with Pope Urban VIII, to ward off predictions that were frightening the Pope.

Throughout Shakespeare's plays there is also a strong theme of Hermetic unity between the natural world and the doings of humanity. In Hamlet, the rotten state of Denmark is signified by 'stars with trains of fire, and dews of blood, disasters in the sun'. The death of Caesar is portended in Act 1, Scene 3 of *Julius Caesar* by a wide-eyed account from Casca of a long list of strange signs he has seen. *Macbeth* is riddled with weird omens, from horses eating each other to the final movement of Birnam Wood to Dunsinane. Storms are especially significant in Shakespearian drama. Always a major symbol of the mysterious power of nature, they undergo a significant change. In *Midsummer Night's Dream* and *Macbeth*, they are the result of fairy trickery and black magic. By the last plays however, storms have become associated with the white magic of the alchemist.

This concept of a synthesised and magically connected world was lost with the Age of Reason. It was replaced by a mechanical, dis-integrated, cause-and-effect model of reality. Hermeticism continued, but as an underground stream. It surfaced again in the 19th century through the Romantic poets, and later the Spiritualist movement. In the 20th century Carl Jung re-established the principle of synchronicity, saying that events occur in similar clusters. This principle of the 'acausal connecting principle' was also upheld by the Chinese, who have interpreted events in terms of meaningful coincidence for thousands of years. Many of Shakespeare's plays, especially *Hamlet*, contain a sense that the events are created by a mind-set rather than cause-and effect.

Pericles was the first of Shakespeare's final set of plays on the theme of learned Hermetic magicians. Throughout his career, Shakespeare's topical allusions were often disguised by similar sounding names. Although the sage in this play was named Cerimon, the character and the word 'Pericles' are both close enough to Paracelsus to invite comparisons. Both were medical practitioners. Both believed more in the secret properties *"that dwell in vegetives, in metals, stones"* than the traditional form of university taught medicine. Cerimon is presented as a good man, not interested in "tottering honour" or "silken bags". Another character praises his charity and generosity, declaring that he has healed hundreds with his knowledge. A fortuitous storm brings some sailors to his house, with a mysterious chest that was washed up on the shore. The chest is opened to reveal the corpse of a Queen. Cerimon brings her back to life, using 'Egyptian magic' for reviving the recently dead.

In *The Winter's Tale*, written soon after *Pericles*, Paulina brings a statue to life with similar magic. To make it clear she is not "assisted by wicked powers" she first obtains the King's sanction to revive his Queen. When it works, he declares "If this be magic, let it be an art lawful as eating."

A Queen being restored to life and able to rejoin the King has alchemical echoes, representing the restoration of the lost divine feminine principle. These symbolic enactments may have been intended as a form of Hermetic ritual, like the masques.

Of the latter scene, Frances Yates comments,

> *"It seems obvious, though I do not think that this has ever been pointed out, that Shakespeare is alluding to the famous god-making passage in the Asclepius."*

The Asclepius was a section of the Corpus Hermetica that described ancient Egyptian magical practices – such as how to restore life to the dead, or turn statues into gods. For the more conservative Hermeticists, this section was questionable because it dealt with magic, and it tended to be played down or excluded. The Italian Giordano Bruno, however, whole-heartedly embraced the entire Corpus.

A rambunctious personality, Bruno came to England in the

1580s, enthusiastically promoting every aspect of Hermetic philosophy. His visit to Oxford in 1583 spawned a flurry of pamphlets on alchemy, Paracelsian medicine and other Hermetic subjects. He established himself as a strong influence in this country, and even hoped to persuade Elizabeth I to bring about universal reform according to Hermetic principles. Although that ambition remained beyond him, his influence can be found in Shakespeare's plays. As well as those illustrations of Asclepian magic, there is also the playwright's Bruno-esque concept of love as a conscious deity, especially in *Love's Labours Lost*. Ulysses' great speech in *Troilus and Cressida* (1.3) is an almost direct expression of Bruno's view of the sun as the physical and spiritual centre of the cosmos.

Bruno's career in England ended when he was tempted back to Italy with the false promise of a wealthy patron. Once there, the Inquisition arrested him. He was executed as an unrepentant heretic in Rome in 1600. Around the same time, John Dee had fallen into deep disfavour with the Queen. His high position and influence at court was over. In 1603 James I began his reign with more stringent laws against witchcraft and magic. The Hermetic movement went steadily underground from around that time, becoming more and more confined to sequestered societies such as the Rosicrucrians.

During that time of gathering clouds, the light of Renaissance philosophy continued to burn in Shakespeare's plays. *Cymbeline*, written in about 1610, was the penultimate of his Hermetic plays. It too featured a magical resurrection after a death-like sleep, this time involving a mysterious cave. An important Rosicrucian symbol is the vault where Christian Rosenkreutz's tomb was found, signifying the revival of lost knowledge. Frances Yates says, *"as far as we know, the earliest date at which the Fama may have been circulating is 1610. Nevertheless, the Rosicrucian manifestoes undoubtedly reflect a movement which was in existence earlier."*

Freemasons today still perform a ritual in which the initiate is 'raised from the dead'. One can only surmise why this symbology should feature so much in Shakespeare's last plays.

There is also the possibility that these coded dramas may in turn have influenced the development of organisations like the Rosicrucians. English acting companies were producing these plays in Germany in the early years of the 17th century. In 1616 *The Chemical Wedding of Christian Rosenkreutz* was published by the German author Andreae, who was so deeply impressed by the Bard of Avon that he also wrote plays 'in imitation of the English dramatists'. These turned out to be mostly copies of Shakespeare's last plays. The connection between those plays and Rosicrucianism is closely woven indeed.

The Tempest was Shakespeare's final expression of magic. Many believe that the character of Prospero is a portrait of John Dee, who like Prospero was a mathematician, astrologer and alchemist. Frances Yates calls The Tempest *"a Rosicrucian manifesto infused with the spirit of Dee, using theatrical parables for esoteric communication."*

The theme of magical storms reaches its apotheosis in this play. The title itself may refer to the alchemical meaning of the term 'tempest': a boiling process to remove impurities from base metal to facilitate its transmutation to gold. Base metal and gold had alchemical meanings connected with personal evolution. Similarly, the 'tempest' of the play meant much more than a heavy storm.

Prospero's island is his own psyche, and also represents society. The drama is about how he brings the conflicting elements on his island into a state of harmony. The wedding in the play is a metaphor for the symbolic alchemical marriage between the 'Prince' and 'Princess' within human nature – the red and white rose. The alchemist's Great Work is on the microcosm of himself, to affect the macrocosm of the world. *The Tempest* is about that process.

The timing of the writing, production and publication of *The Tempest* was dramatic in itself. By that time, attitudes to magic had hardened. Witch hunting fever was beginning to stalk the land, and this included Hermeticists. Rejected by both monarchs, John Dee died in great poverty in 1608. *The Tempest* was written and produced a year or two later. It was quite likely Shakespeare's declaration of allegiance for all that Dee represented. With James I on the throne hostile to the occult in general and John Dee in particular, the production of *The Tempest* was an act of political courage.

After Shakespeare himself died in 1616, his theatre company, The King's Men, organised the first folio publication of his collected works. The plays had been published individually, but only in unbound little quartos, of the ephemeral and trashy end of the market. A folio publication was the large impressive form reserved for established works of merit. *The Tempest* was significantly placed at the front of this first folio collection of 1623.

In the same year, Bacon's *De Augmentis Scientarum* was also published. This was the philosophical background and purpose of Shakespeare's plays - the key to unlock their esoteric meaning. A year later in 1624, the cipher book *Cryptomenytices* came out, providing the cipher keys to encoded Rosicrucian references in Shakespeare's plays and poetry.

Although the Bard's works do stand alone as supreme literary achievements, a fuller understanding of them can only be gained by appreciating the philosophy of the esoteric codes and symbols that are embedded in the stories.

The hopeful magic of Hermetic theatricals might seem to have been defeated by the dark times that followed in the 17th century. And yet, nearly five hundred years later, *The Tempest* is still produced for entertainment as well as study; and the concept of wise, benign magic has returned to life in Tolkein's Gandalf, ObiWan Kenobi of Star Wars, and Harry Potter's Professor Dumbledore.

The name 'Prospero' means 'hope for the future'. Through powerful modern media, the spirit of Prospero and all he stood for now strides the macrocosm of the globe in ways that even Shakespeare would not have imagined.

The Lincoln Cathedral Code – Solution to the Mystery of Rennes-Le-Chateau?
By Callum Jensen

Rennes-le-Chateau is indeed, to my enquiring and scientific mind, a strange place. Like others on the world map, I have this feeling that it draws certain individuals to it, like blood cells in a body rushing to an internal part of the anatomy, or anti-bodies on their way to a diseased area. In my own experiences, Glastonbury Tor and the Scottish island of Iona are two such other places that afford this subtle 'calling'. It may even be that certain geographical areas – imagine them, as spots on a physical human body - have to be visited in a specific order, to achieve a something cosmic, which we as mere mortals can never understand. Maybe these places are the cosmic equivalent of acupuncture points on the Earth's living body.... maybe we have to dig or excavate them to provide the equivalent of a microsurgical operation? Before my involvement with RLC, I recall having first visited Malta (where the Knights Templar originated) and her megalithic temples, the Carles stone circle at Keswick, Cumbria, England, the chalk giant of Dorset, the Tor and Iona. On all occasions I was never truly sure what I was doing there! Later, I was to discover that all these strategic places had one hidden thing in common - fertility and pregnancy. A birth in the offing, somewhere? I went to RLC for the first and only time in April of 1986, the year that ominous Halley's comet passed us by that February. The previous year I had some interesting exchange with geometrician David Wood who had shocked a great many Rennes readers with his privately published 'GenIsis'. It seems I was never fated to work with David - circumstances kept us apart after a while, including a transgression by authoress Elizabeth Van Buren who lived in the Rennes Valley and whom David placed much faith in.

My wife and I appeared to have a tryst or, as David would call it, a date calculation, with the valley. I had received it in a dream, 24th April as well as the word 'lacombe'. As a neurologist who prefers to believe that all the mysteries known to Man could be explained by that mystifying and private computer we call the brain if only it would confide us instead of allowing us to live our lives out using only an allocated one-fifth of it, I accept that accurate 'messages' can be relayed in the dream state, so April 24th it was! We were greeted upon our entrance into the Valley a week or so earlier at around 8.20 in the evening, by the sudden appearance of a rainbow!

Aerial phenomenon appears to be a facet of the area - sudden and strategic solitary thunderclaps a speciality! If Lovelock has it right with his Gaia Theory, this could be an explanation - if the planet is a living, breathing intelligence (as I believe also), then it could conjure up these things by thought. Cosmic, I know, and near impossible to prove. A French chap who had the 'calling' had built himself his own Navaho-style stone hut to live in the Valley. He was called Daniel, and circumstances led us to him, which was convenient, as he had moved to RLC to await the arrival of two specific people. Daniel was convinced it was us. The name he had given his hut - 'Lacombe'.

There was to be a lunar eclipse at 1.24 the afternoon of the 24th, not that we would see it in France. Again, circumstances dictated that we were placed in a certain position within the Valley for that time, close to Green Rocks. I recall how before we had left, we had told David Wood that the Rennes Valley was a 'Time Clock'. It sure is precise! Minus Daniel, we had had an adventure even earlier that day. One of those strange single thunderclaps had led us to a rock cropped tomb. Holding a copy of GenIsis in our hands, we could see that this tomb had been painted exactly by Leonardo Da Vinci in one of his paintings of *'The Virgin of the Rocks'*...the one where Mary is without halo. It is at the top of the painting! This tomb appeared to have two points of entry both sealed by rubble, and appearing to head subterranean. I think it is painted by Teniers in his *'Temptation of St Anthony'* from another angle. There was also a niche that gave the impression that it was for the votive placing of flowers. An upright stone 'marker' was nearby, too. Afterwards when we mentioned the site to Daniel, he told us how once he had seen two people digging there, and Van Buren told us it was her 'special place' where she would visit and sprinkle holy water. David knew of it, too. And so, I think it is safe to say that there IS something in all this Da Vinci Code stuff after all! Nobody to my knowledge has ever mentioned this site in publication. My feelings are that here was ONCE the sanctuary/hiding place/final resting place of Mary Magdalene, until being moved at a later date to England, watched over by Knights Templar.... hence the importance of RLC who once had this most special treasure hidden in its Valley, clues left at a later date by Berenger Sauniere to hint at exactly where she had been removed to. It was my wife who was 'led' to this tomb discovery with one of those timely, single thunderclaps. (Once, when unsure which direction to follow and pointing with his hand, A clap 'led' David Wood to a place of specific geometry) She has the neurological condition known as 'high functioning autism' – a sort of different brain wiring from the norm - and leads her life through signs and symbols. Upon reaching the tomb, she fell to her knees sobbing and exclaiming 'Atoora', over and over. We have never actually found what this word or name might be, or in what language, but she feels it has something to do with the aorta - or heart. It is interesting that she can 'read' the strange language of Boudet with her autism, too...the Green language of Fulcanelli. Other very unlikely incidents during our time in the Valley included photographing a strange giant protoplasmic or biological cell rising up from the Poussin tomb at Arques, and a ghostly Knight sitting on a horse in Sauniere's garden...he was even smiling at the camera!! Although we now no longer have these amazing photographs, lost in a caravan theft in 2000, I did send the tomb cell photo to both 33 degree Freemasonic Lodges of England and Scotland as part of a dossier in 1989, anonymously. Perhaps it still exists with them. Arguably the weirdest and yet most straightforward of our encounters was reserved for the evening of April 24th 1986, at about 8pm. The evening was light and warm, and there was myself, my wife and her son (my stepson, who was only 14 at the time), along with Daniel and his dog Sappho in his stone hut. Collectively, we were all fairly tired after a hot day exploring about in the Valley, sometimes together, others times separately, and enjoying a rest. Me, the wife and our boy were living adjacent the hut in a large mobile caravan. It was Rene who first spotted the three bright lights far in the distance, high up in the cloudless sky. We all watched them, bright like stars and almost in a straight line with an equal distance between them, fixed and motionless. It is as if they had appeared from out of nowhere. Almost at once, we all realised that these lights were now slowly moving towards us, and then, as easily as they had arrived, they vanished from sight...to be replaced by a huge formed cloud, flashing amber from within its density. Electrical flashes began to emanate from it, no thunder, just the flashes like lightning. I can only imagine an electrical storm is something similar. The atmosphere was quite eerie as everything else in the Valley was still and soundless and not a single soul in sight outside of the four of us. It was as if Time had stood still. At a later date I drew the comparison with the biblical description in Ezekiel of a storm coming from out of the East, and also with the description of British authoress Jenny Randles in her book entitled 'Time storms'. Daniel's dog was frantic throughout as we watched how this strange flashing amber cloud drifted across the Valley, over us and off to sail around the back of Rennes-le-Chateau. Surely existing villagers who are still living there today must have remembered this evening of 24th April 1986. I will always remember how it was Daniel - who apparently still lives in the area today, and has been blamed as the fellow who in recent years chopped off and stole the original devil statue's head - who broke the silence announcing, 'I think it was a spaceship...' Years after the event, I realised a few synchronicities concerning this encounter. In the classic Steven Spielberg Ufo movie 'Close encounters of the third kind' (screened in 1977), the name of the French scientist who first witnessed contact with the aliens - and I suspect he was styled on widely respected French astrophysicist and Ufo researcher Jacques Vallee - was Lacombe...the name Daniel has ascribed to his home and which I had received in a dream. In the movie, the contact was made by rendezvous with a select few who had little choice in eventually finding themselves at a place called 'Devil's Tower' which is an actual place at Wyoming, USA. A title that has often being attributed to the Tower Magdala at RLC is...the Devil's Tower! How Spielberg in his movie showed the forming of a huge cloud that contained a Ufo within was disturbing for us to watch when we first saw the movie in 1990 - it was so reminiscent of what we had watched in the sky above Rennes that evening. That night, after the event had subsided, my wife had a bad dream and within it came a clear message, which said, 'When the bird leaves it's nest, look to the West.' In the dream she saw how we were being pursued by an angry lynch mob and so we took it as a sign that it was time to leave the strangeness of the Valley, returning to England. Before we left, we called on Van Buren to see what she had thought, only to be informed that she had left the Valley the previous day and would be away for weeks. Within 36 hours of our encounter with the strange amber cloud the nuclear reactor at Chernobyl had exploded releasing radiation into the atmosphere, which, in time, polluted much of Russia and has sailed around the world.

There is another bizarre factor which may contribute to our puzzling interaction with our event. Earlier that day, my wife and I had travelled to the small church of Bugarach not too far from

RLC. Again, it seems to have been one of those occasions whereby you do not fully understand why you are visiting a place. I waited outside as my wife requested that she went into the church alone. When she came back out after a short while, she was most perplexed and explained that when she went in there she suddenly burst into what she could best describe as singing opera at the top of her voice, something she had never done in her life, let alone wonder if she were capable. It is as if we had gone there just for her to have this unexpected vocal outburst. This is made all the stranger with the knowledge that Berenger Sauniere befriended famed opera singer Emma Calve, and it is rumoured he would have her sing opera at the Chateau under specific and arranged circumstances, only the pair of them present. My wife has since concerned herself when she read the part in the Book of Revelations that says how an angel appeared holding the key to the bottomless pit, and feels that this may be a reference to her singing in the unknown musical key at the Bugarach church, in some way it relating to the release of the strange amber cloud and anything else it may have contained. Was it on a time ordained mission? Am I to really think that we may have played a part in Revelations? It is unthinkable, and certainly not the sort of thing one would hope to be involved in, even if it is at all possible.

When we returned back to Lincoln, England, dazed and confused from our experiences, we had little further to do with RLC, and not particularly wishing to either. Even to this day my stepson cannot fathom or understand what he saw that fateful evening and it has most certainly shaped his outlook on life. For the next phase of this true story, we must fast-forward ahead some almost twenty years, and to 'The Lincoln Da Vinci Code'...

Lincoln, I now realise, had always drawn me to it. I first came down from the North East of England in 1979, missing my wife to be by a matter of weeks as she left there to live in the USA. We finally did connect in 1984, and Lincoln was never far from the picture, until we returned there to settle in 1998. Lincoln Cathedral, the famous Gothic Cathedral that sits high up a hill and had a church dedicated to Mary Magdalene demolished in 1067 to make way for it, has already had a controversial past, a sex scandal at the turn of the century and in 1995 a public declaration by the then Dean announcing that he believed a battle between good and evil was centred there and he wished to have the Cathedral closed for three months to have it exorcised! What could he have meant? Not the sort of thing you would expect to be associated with such an edifice, and even today, he will not elucidate further. My story took an unexpected twist in April 2005 when a glazer accidentally made an astonishing discovery whilst cleaning stain glass at the scene of The Last Supper at the Great East Window. There are 64 roundels there, each telling a biblical story and high enough up to go undetected by the eye (and unnoticed since its inception in 1885) compounded by the fact that it is quite small, he found on Christ's platter neither cup nor bread, but a DOG!

The argument is that it is a paschal lamb, but when you consider that a short distance away this exact dog appears again at a 15th century woodcut of a station of the cross looking up at Jesus, and within the precincts of the Cathedral there is a similar dog accompanying Lord Tennyson, famed Grail poet, as part of his 1903 statue, you begin to take the hint! The dog was a symbol used by Freemasons when their early meetings were considered illegal, and of course, it is associated with Sirius, the Dog Star. A 'Star Clock' has also been discovered within the Cathedral at the Rose Window, a planisphere of the Northern Constellations. I found many, many other anomalies within and around the Cathedral that interlocked to provide what was obviously a Code and 'paper chase.' Researching into the local history of the area and of the Cathedral, bit by bit this code began to unfold, until it led to a final spot and conclusion. Confirmation that we were on a trail occurred when the famous and unsolved controversial RLC Parchments began to reveal themselves at Lincoln, the indication being that they appeared to be based on architecture and features within the Cathedral. The Tennyson statue, too, decoded Parchment 2 with its cryptic plaques awaiting discovery. The phenomenon of 'drawing' people to an area continued, when Hollywood, no less, visited Lincoln Cathedral to film scenes for the screen version of Dan Brown's 'The Da Vinci Code'. Amazing! Synchronicities began to pour in reminding us that the name of the man who started all this Grail stuff back in the 70's is Henry Lincoln! The name on the crucial 'marker tomb' where the Code led us is one and the same as the QC who defended Baigent and Leigh against Dan Brown in the London Courts! The very week Hollywood were filming, electrical cable needed laying to provide power for the rigging lights and when workmen began digging the lawned area in the front of the South East corner of the South west transept, they found a tomb containing the bones of a decapitated unknown woman! Situated in a very unusual place and a total surprise to, and unrecorded by, the Cathedral who new nothing of it being there, archaeologists quickly dated it as being from the 14/15th century. Only a few hundred yards away from the Lincoln Da Vinci Code marker tomb, under which we may be going to find the lost treasure of the Templars, little did the Cathedral know that this tomb is the decoy in the Quest, deliberately contrived to lead searchers to thinking that this was the hinted at lost tomb in the area, the secret of the Cathedral over which good and evil were in a struggle.

Not only do the RLC parchments decode fully here, but so too does the bas relief of the Magdalene, placed above the altar at the RLC church. Although full, exhaustive explanations are given in my two books 'The Lincoln Da Vinci Code' and 'The Lincoln Da Vinci Code and the mystery of Rennes-le-Chateau', I will briefly run through the unravelling, as they presented themselves to me - many more clues revealed as well as these RLC contributions. Shepherdess, no temptation...alludes to the pregnant (although nobody spotted this until I announced it) statue Queen Eleanor high up on the Cathedral SE buttress, who stares over at the marker tomb within the St Margaret burial grounds. St Margaret was a shepherdess whose life ended in decapitation. Strangely for a virgin, she had been venerated for centuries as patron of pregnant women. The shepherdess in the Poussin painting is pregnant, too, if you look closely, therefore, sexually, no temptation! That Poussin and Teniers hold the key peace, there is a painting by Teniers entitled 'The Cabinet of Archduke Leopold'. It contains over 50 paintings within the one. The centrepiece is of St Margaret, seen with a green drape hanging over the top right of her frame. The place name of where the St Margaret burial grounds are located...The Green! Not only does the French word 'tenure' mean 'to hold', here we are looking at the meaning of the word hold as in 'to aim, to direct'...for the pregnant statue on the corner looks directly over at the marker tomb in the grounds. Her gaze is holding the key peace/piece, directionally. 681 is a reference to the Cathedral's Sun Dial, thirty foot up the buttress of the SE corner of the Transept...its numerals 6,8 and 1 are equally spaced in a peculiar fashion. By the cross and this horse of God, is found inside the Cathedral at the Choir Stalls, a carved depiction of a knight falling from his horse.

The horse has its legs crossed. I complete this guardian demon... refers to the famous Lincoln Imp carved high upon the North side of the Angel Choir. This 13th century marker being the original demon within the church, Sauniere having made his own version. (The origin of the word 'imp', I traced back to meaning 'Sion'!) To complete him, we return to the sundial where we find the Latin motto 'Pereunt et Imputantur'...'imp' being completed as 'imputantur'. At Mid-day blue apples refers to the fact that at noon on 22nd July, Feast of the Magdalene, when the sun is at its height, its rays strike down and through a blue and red section of the central pane next to pregnant Eleanor to create a dappling effect on the floor of the Cathedral resembling blue apples. I checked this only this year - firstly a blue patch falls on the stone floor, quickly followed by two red 'apples' that appear two yards away, as the blue forms into circular 'apples', these red ones jump over to mingle and join them, replaced again by a further two red. At approximately 11.30 that same morning, half an hour before this spectacle, I also managed to fortuitously photograph some Ufo's over the Cathedral that showed themselves for the briefest of seconds!

To explain Parchment 2 we visit the Tennyson statue where

we find the words 'Roi' which is French for 'King', and 'Sion', that interlock acrostic style, to hint at 'King and for Sion is this treasure and it is death'. The St Margaret's burial grounds which indicates a likely lost treasure, are only a few hundred yards away from here – where else would you expect to find death other than at a burial ground?

Finally, amongst too many clues and explanations to mention here, I will tackle the Magdalene bas-relief. The Magdalene has alongside side her the decapitated skull of Margaret. If you draw a straight line through her eye level and continue through the centre of her cross, you will see that the line hits on the 28th tomb shaped inner design. Returning briefly to the cross and horse of God, if you count the number of fastenings on the right of the horse you will find 7, on the left side 4. Multiply (or x) these to arrive also at 28. The number of the plot where we arrive at the marker tomb at the burial grounds is indexed as....28!! If you take a look at the feature on the far left of the bas-relief, you can compare it with Lincoln Castle - it is exact, and if you stand at the spot of the LDVC marker tomb this is exactly where you will see and view it. EXACTLY!

Thus ends the Lincoln Da Vinci Code, and my twenty-year mainly unwanted association with Rennes-le-Chateau. Are the

Grail/ Mary and her secrets under the marker tomb? Well, this spot is precisely where once stood the church of St Margaret, demolished in 1781, the very year that Marie de Negre died. Ten years after, Abbe Bigou erected slabs to reinstate the clue that has been lost with the demolition of the church and Marie's death, for below this spot the lost church crypt still hides. My decoding of the Negre slabs reveal 'St Margaret's at Lincoln, 8' down '- you can see the full working out on my website. What are the odds of a hidden Cathedral code leading to an exact spot where there are no traces that a church once ever stood? And companion clues leading here from clues left in France by Berenger Sauniere who must have known that the RLC treasure was actually in England. Am I truly the only person to have found where Mary was once hid and now where she has been relocated? The Cathedral is to grant me a GPR scan at the precise location in Spring 2007. We may not have long to wait and see.

The Lincoln Cathedral Code – Solution to the Mystery of Rennes-Le-Chateau? An Update By Callum Jensen

Since this feature originally appeared in The Temple magazine, my already controversial Lincoln Cathedral Code took a further dramatic twist when the Cathedral authorities reneged on their previous agreement to allow a Ground Penetrating Radar scan at the concluded location, closing ranks with little in the way of explanation. My efforts to involve the Archbishop of Canterbury brought no joy, only the understanding of a protocol that says that not even the Archbishop can intervene or overturn internal decisions made within a Cathedral.

This unexpected U-turn was made all the more frustrating as I had by then added further weighty evidence for my conclusion by way of solving the undecoded Marie de Negre headstone for it to read 'Margaret at Lincoln', and by demonstrating how Andre Douzet's model map maquette reveals the topography of the city of Lincoln as easily as anywhere in France, and further confirms my precise location. I had also received the combination of cast iron mathematical, astronomical and computer confirmation that Lincoln Cathedral in its position on the ground reflects the star Arcturus - origin of the King Arthur myths - and how at midday on 17th January, a major factor in the Rennes mystery, the Cathedral altar directly faces the star.

However, a glimmer of hope returned when a fortuitous chance encounter reinforced the rumour of a tunnel hidden somewhere in the Bishops Palace, adjacent the Cathedral, thought to lead to a nearby crypt. To my surprise and investigation, the Palace confirmed this historical rumour to me personally! Having located and accessed one such speculative point of entry, my venture was recorded by a film crew and will be featured in the forthcoming *'The Lincoln Cathedral Da Vinci Code'* DVD, released Autumn 2009.

A letter from Rieux, Minervois
By Stephen Andrews

After many promises I have started to write about my Templar travels and so I thought I would start with some thoughts about my latest "find". Before launching into the explanation of the wonderful tale of how I came upon the singularly beautiful rotunda church in Rieux - Minervois, I think it only right that I establish my limited credentials and try to explain how I came to be in France and how this relates to our shared love of the Temple.

I have wandered the main roads and by-ways of Europe since finding the Holy Blood and the Holy Grail in 1981, in the back of a car I was driving purely by chance. The book rekindled a spark that had been set aside in favour of "serious" study for my career in the honourable profession of Town Planning and Conservation. It seemed such a chore at the time, but the knowledge I gained as a planning student has given me a firm base for my searches and observations ever since.

The small fire rekindled was first lit by The Knights of the

Temple in the Television programmes of the early 1960s when Roger Moore played Ivanhoe and Richard Greene was the definitive Robin Hood. I tried to read Ivanhoe in the "Dean's" children's book version but it wasn't as much fun as laid-on-a-plate Ivanhoe from ITV but I enjoyed every detail about the Knights with the blood red cross on the white top and they seemed to be the heroes when the anti heroes dressed in black or had sinister helmets with wings to identify them. I am now reading the tale of Ivanhoe in more detail but that is for another time.

It has been nearly a quarter of a century now - of course I have been drawn into the Rennes le Chateau story (- that is, after all, how I restarted) but I soon came to realise that with the breadth of fascinating material on the widest range of historical, alchemical and downright fantastical I would need to keep refocusing on the task at hand. I chose to follow the Temple. It has taken me, and my ever loyal family, through the most wonderful and remote parts of England Scotland and Ireland then to France Italy and several years ago to Tomar and Santiago de Compostella. Fiona and the boys have now accepted that they have been places and seen things that many will not have seen and begrudgingly they accept that Gozo and the Sierra Verde beat Ibetha every time.

Following the site references in *The Holy Blood Holy Grail* I guess I should have realised earlier on that I was indeed travelling the Pilgrim routes that had been followed by my heroes. The people and "chattels" the Templars conveyed and protected around the roman roads and tracks needed to be understood. I knew there was a deeper understanding to be gained of a turbulent and sometimes tragic period of history. Maybe my developing understanding of buildings and how they were built, ordered and altered would help me in this quest. It was to lead to some of the most wondrous and perhaps sacred countryside in Europe and if I have supped of the Grail it may simply have been the enjoyment of these wonderful off centre, out of the way, places of peace and tranquillity that fed me what I needed in my own troubled times. But Hey! - that's life and this is an article about the wondrous church of the St Mairie not an auto biography. The discipline of report writing must take over...

The square in Mirepoix is always the place to sit and watch the French watching the English taking their recreation. I had just secured a copy of the Yellow Cross by Rene Weis (another Cathar history book) and I was viewing the carved joist ends of the jetties that project over one corner of the square. You know them when you see them - and see them you must!

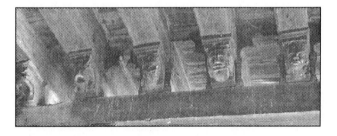

A young grandmother approached the carved heads and began an explanation for a wide eyed seven-ish grand daughter. Collette was clearly informed and passionate about her subject and I wanted to tell her of the similar heads that can be seen elsewhere in France and under the eaves of Roslin chapel. My broken French was succeeding just when her son arrived - to act as a very able interpreter. We were able to exchange some ideas and she explained that she had brought her granddaughter to see the heads as they were just like those that could be found in her church at Riuex - Minervois. Like a tramp on a kipper I instinctively knew that a visit was a must and the son set down Collete's name and the Church address for me to find as we parted. I knew Collette was a kind and generous person and so it proved.

Rieux Minervois lies in the heart of Cathar country. Make

your way to Carcassone - look for the sign post for Mazamet to leave the town to the North on the D118 and after say 1mile start to look for the road going right onto the D620 (signposted Caunes-Minervois) after another 10 miles (generally to the NE with the forboding Montagne Noires on your left ghastly grey with clouds every time I've seen them) Follow the road D11 to the South East for the linked villages of Peyriac and Rieux - Minervois. Plenty of parking in the square and side roads but park up as walking around the church area will give you a sense of the place and the shape of the old cathar town. It felt like the small, so called, "Templar" town of Compagne sur Aude.

The whole wonderful edifice has been dated to the second half of the 12th Century and surprise, surprise, - it is sited on top of a much earlier church. I would wager for a temple being present before that. The English translator on my computer charmingly suggests "on the place of a previous church no more tracks of which there are". I know just what the computer meant as worryingly some of my sentences this way come out. Don't forget your proximity in this location to the southern exit of the Black Mountains. The early Burgundians making their way south from Bjornholm are well placed to be bringing their brand of Christianity south and as we shall see below the Burgundian connection will become important.

The entrance to the church is usually open although after the sad theft of the chandeliers, that were situated on either side of the alter, the church is often locked from midi to 2.00p.m. After your lunch - there are a number of excellent restaurants in walking distance - you need to visit the Syndicate d'Initiative and speak to the lovely Collette Cuxzac and her, English-speaking, chum the equally lovely Edith. If you are visiting in the normal hours then do not be put off by the small door in one of the seven sides opposite the main door it is always kept locked - it is the door of the Midday sun(!) - caution though that's my translation.

The church of St Mary the Virgin has a polygonal plan with 14 wall segments surrounding the heptagonal sanctuary. Yes, that is indeed seven - sided building techniques. Now I know that the art of brick rubbing is alive and well and that concrete can be cast into pretty much any shape angle or form but the mastery over the geometry and control over the forms is breathtaking in its execution. I thought that I was being condescending to our forbears who were so skilled to be able to do these things as far back as 1150 - 1200. Then I reminded myself that the geometry had been available for thousands of years and I was indeed thinking like a modern elitist. Nonetheless, this is the only Seven sided church known in the Languedoc and until someone tells her otherwise Collette thinks it is the only one in the world.

Interestingly, the Syndacat web site says that the number seven symbolises the wisdom of Mary. I'm sure they are right but maybe we owe as much to the wisdom of the Masons for the interior we behold still today. If so the importance of the seven in the form of the liberal arts and sciences may be the more salient issue. The beauty of the seven columns is worth the trip alone. Three round or cylindrical pillars interspersed by 4 square (more properly called prismic) pillars. The three round pillars form the triangle of the skies (or some local pundits say the gods or spirit) and the Prismic pillars form the square of the earth and represent the physical condition or the world of matter. Over the wonderful Caunes stone alter the ceiling of the chapel comes to a perfectly circular conclusion with the centre dominated with a stylised red cross...

The interior is marked by the regularity of the geometry and the 14 quarter circle top arches that rest on floriated and decorated capitals - some bedecked with palm trunks and foliage, others with heads and bugle-snorting rapscallions of the sort you see in a Hieronymous Bosch painting, waiting to torment the falling sinners. These wee folk are situated in the anteroom or chapel that now, due to later alterations, houses the organ. They sit on the capitals of the pillars of the original Romanesque door at the porch way or entrance to the chapel.

The importance of this original doorway cannot be underesti-mated as the chapel which now encloses it also conceals a fun little chap that we must concentrate on further in a moment.

My guide and co traveller in the strange world of the carved heads had been so excited to see me. I was a stranger that she knew perhaps - but one that she had passed in the square of Mirepoix. From the first time we met I knew that she was keen to impart her knowledge. When I withdrew from our conversation in Mirepoix, it was because of my French - not a lack of willingness to continue. There was another reason. Having seen the reaction of my boys to my history, over the last 15 years, I didn't want another young impressionable person turned off to history...and that was Collettes' son or Son in Law! - the grandchild would be permanently scarred and turned off history forever!!

When I departed with all the courtesy I could muster and the promise "a bientot", her wish to see me visit Rieux was almost tangible. She clearly had hoped that we would visit to enjoy the benefits of St Mairie. So poor old gal - when she realised Les Anglais had made the effort, she was at once excited and amazed and keen to ensure we had the best of attention. Once the initial shock had subsided she asked Edith to accompany us to the church to ensure a guide could help in English. SO when you go to Rieux, ask for Collette and say Stephen sent you for a warm welcome from the best part of France. As you know, Oddvar and dear reader, it is the people you meet on your journey that make the journey. Just pray they are good folk.

Back to my fun little man in the porch way.

Remember that the roman arch would have been the original doorway into the seven pillared temple that originally existed on the site. (A Romanesque door into a possibly pagan temple site perhaps?) The construction of the outer walls offered the opportunity to enclose and perhaps protect the beauty of what existed there before. This interesting little chap has been crafted on top of the pillar facing the roman arch on the later outside wall. Collette gave her "explanation" of the character. The Maitre de Cabestany - a fabled master of Masonry - has carved capitals and chapters all across the pilgrimage crescent stretching from Compostella through Southern France across to Northern Italy. In this case he had carved this fellow to represent avarice and the serpents of the devil were gnawing at his ears for ever.

Look more closely, and apart from the serpents we can see a man with a beard who has a pair of full length tongs slung from his shoulders down his chest that he is using to carry a vat or crucible. Is the crucible being used for the transmuting of gold from base metals (a reference to alchemy - the great work) or is it carrying the molten brass for the castings of the pillars at the porch way or entrance of King Solomon's temple. Hiram Abiff was the superintendent responsible for their casting - and much more of the Temple at Jerusalem. Either way, the character has been hidden in the upper corner of the anteroom and judging by the residual plaster that covers it and other reliefs in the chapel they have been at some time lime washed to cover their detailing. Now, fortunately they have been cleaned and made presentable for a new generation to view.

The Temple connection is furthered by these serpents - if you visit the round church of Northampton you will find a similar looking little chap again with a "serpent" attending close at hand. Because of the Temple connection and the working tools which Hiram has close at hand I was of the opinion that the serpents were not snakes but the Shamir or worm that crunched his way through the joints between the stones of the Temple. (No metal instruments were allowed to profane the process of construction) Surely, the serpent portrayed in most of history is long, curly and several bends, like the snakes entwining the caduceus. Both of these characters - like the worm of Northampton have a single bend, a fat belly and a limited length. Perhaps the serpent Rouge found in the foothills of the Pyrenees is a similar tradition to a similar snake tale found near at hand. Not far away the local war lord allegedly descended into the mountains surrounding Perrillos in the Corbieres to find seek and destroy the Devils' snake that frequents the underground caves. The snake / worm motif needs further research and comment - so let me know if you can help.

Whoever this character may be he is overseen by a later statue of St James dressed in pilgrim's garb. He is also spattered with the lime of a previous era that covered him. It is as if the Pilgrim's saint is counteracting a perceived evil from the ancient temple.

Finally, in this most interesting of churches the final curiosity. An extraordinary relief version of the interment of Jesus. Edith from the syndicat d'initiative suggested that the carving was of the "Burgundian" style. Now I am not sure what this means to a French art critic but the carving followed the format of having been recently cleaned and restored as if again painted over by previous generations to conceal the content in the colours in some way.

A friend of yours Oddvar may be able to say more about this relief - I think you said Nicodemus at one end of the proceedings and Joseph of Arimethea at the other- surely too many people to be orthodox though. Five women with very dark skin behind the body of Jesus and a third man!? In this strange portrayal two other Templar style details are notable. Firstly, no lance wound hole is visible -miraculously healed perhaps or is the relief saying something to us like the Jesus of Tomar...and Secondly, the whole panel is set within the same sort of semicircular shaped niche that the Templar knights were often laid out in, to rest.

The French writer Andre Bonnery in the "Master of Cabestany" suggests that the number seven can return our thoughts to the worship of Mary - going back to her early association with Wisdom. Proverbs Ch9 says " *Wisdom hath builded her house - she hath hewn out her seven pillars.*" Perhaps these are truly the seven pillars of wisdom.

The Capital with Mary "in Majesty" speaks of other more ancient symbology and I left the Eglise thinking that I had seen the Queen of the Earth (Gaia) stare out serenely over them. One of the web sites offers the following origins for construction. The local tradition would like the site devoted to Minerva. Others think it is the site of a vast tomb or the baptistery of the 6[th]Century. For what its worth, I think the Hiram emblem on the porch chapiter falls into place with the Templar families return from the site of the Temple with their enriched knowledge. They recognised the importance of the seven-sided Temple and sought to protect it with an external and possibly defensible outer wall. Their take on the humanity of Jesus was reflected in the Burgundian relief.

Despite the sense of wonderment there was also a feeling of immense calm and tranquillity. So, if on the way home you see the white dove "Collombe de Minervois" do not be surprised. It represents the Spiritual side of the Cathar creed and is seen as lapel badges jewellery and carved stones all over the region. Maybe this is the way that the Collombe gets into your mind's-eye. But if, dear reader, you are there and have a fortunate sighting of this fabled bird do tell me as you will have been truly blessed by the perfected. Maybe Collette helped you and me to find a rare bird indeed...?

Poussin and the Sacred Angle
By Jim Beck

"He and I discussed certain things, which I shall with ease be able to explain to you in detail - things which will give you, through Monsieur Poussin, advantages which even kings would have great pains to draw from him, and which, according to him, it is possible that nobody else will ever discover in the centuries to come. And what is more, these are things so difficult to discover that nothing now on this earth can prove of better fortune nor be their equal."
Louis Fouquet - writing to his brother.

A 17th century artist, by the name of Nicolas Poussin, is believed by many to hold the keys to unlocking the secrets found buried in the history of Rennes-le-Chateau, the actions of a certain parish priest, and the myths and legends of the surrounding area. It is also believed that the solutions to these secrets are in someway encoded within his works of art. One such work, "The Shepherds of Arcadia", has received the majority of the attention in this regard, mainly for the following reasons: 1) Decoded in one the the parchments, purportedly discovered by a parish priest at the church of Rennes-le-Chateau, is the phrase **"Shepherdess no temptation which Poussin and Teniers hold the key "**. 2) After finding this parchment the priest, allegedly, traveled to Paris to view this and a few other works of art. 3) It is said that King Louis XIV went out of his way to try and acquire this very painting after a cryptic letter had been received by his superintendent of finance Nicolas Fouquet, from his brother, discussing a conversation he had with Nicolas Poussin. It is claimed that, shortly after Fouquet received this letter, King Louis had him arrested and imprisoned for life, never allowing him to speak with anyone.

I have outlined, in a previous article, my reasons for believing this painting does, in fact, hide a key for unlocking at least one small portion of this puzzle. This "key" is in the form of a direction, and when used in conjunction with other information encoded in the parchment, leads to a specific location. Unfortunately, although this location has already been suspect for quite some time, it is not going to be excavated anytime soon. This is not to say that I believe, whatever it was that may have been hidden at this location is actually still there. After all, nowadays there are plenty of better places to store valuable items other than underground vaults or secret tombs. Exactly what was once hidden at this secret location is still anyones guess. Thus far, all I have been able to extract from Poussin is a possible location. The question remains, was Poussin simply encoding the location of this secret for somebody else, or did he also know the nature of what was being hidden? Knowing Poussin's personal insignia, "Tenet Confidentiam", along with his mysterious conversation with Nicolas Fouquet's brother, leads me to the belief, he must have known, "in detail", exactly what this great secret was. Now the question becomes, did he leave behind any clues of this arcane knowledge in his work?

To begin searching Poussin's other paintings for clues, as to what he may have known, it is first important to get somewhat of an idea of just what it is, I might be looking for. Most people are of the belief that this entire mystery centers around a possibility of there existing certain proof, in one form or another, that once exposed, would do great harm to the many Christian based religions. The most widely accepted theory is that this proof consists of evidence that could prove Jesus was married and possibly fathered a child. Another theory contends that Jesus had a twin brother, and that it was not he who died on the cross, rather his twin. Of course, It is easy to imagine how proof of either of these scenarios could be damaging to the Christian faith. Not only would it call in to question the divinity of Jesus, of which the religions are based, but it would also expose the Bible as being a false document, written with the intent to manipulate rather then to disseminate, the truth. It is for this reason it is said , that the secret is so well guarded, because the church would do anything within its power to have it destroyed.

Using these theories as a guide, I began examining some of Poussin's other works. I quickly came across one very promising piece called, "The Institution of the Eucharist", painted around 1640. Interesting enough, it was this very same theme in which Leonardo da Vinci had used to hide his secret knowledge of these very subjects 150 years earlier (see davincisecrets.com for details). In any case, I began my analysis of this painting by first juxtaposing a set of gridlines over the top of the image. Many artists, both past and present, use a grid system in laying out their work as a means in helping them achieve balance in their scene and for determining such aspects as depth and perspective. Upon doing this, I quickly came to the realization that two of the figures depicted were placed on the exact same horizontal plane. Closer examination revealed, not only were they painted on the same level but, also in fact, given the same identical facial features.

It was as though Poussin painted one as a mirror image of the other and this reflection was that of the central figure, Jesus Christ. Once making this revelation, it becomes increasingly clear that Poussin had secretly included a "twin" of Christ in this work. By intentionally placing this second Christ in the shadows, a relatively far distance away from the main Christ figure, Poussin has been able to somehow keep him hidden for all this time. Seeing this, one other aspect in this composition now becomes clear, that being the symbolic nature of the particular type of lantern Poussin had decided to include in this scene. The lantern curiously contains two flames. The flame on the right is burning brighter but looks to be flickering. As for the other, on the left, it is steady and clear. I will leave it up to the viewer as to how best to interpret this.

Continuing my analysis of this painting, I thought it would be important to determine if there was any perspective elements to be identified in the layout of the room in which the scene was taking place. Poussin has rarely used such compositional effects in his other works and there is only a faint trace of him having utilized them here. A careful examination of the various features making up this room revealed the inclusion of a vanishing point. Poussin somewhat attempts to hide this point, his reason for this, I can only assume, is to avoid drawing to much attention to this area. He accomplishes this by using orthogonal lines, located in the ceiling structure and the tiles making up the floor, that are relatively short and far away from the actual vanishing point itself (see gray lines) and by using lighting effects to draw the viewers focus elsewhere.

By extending these orthogonal lines to their point of inter-section, it becomes apparent that they converge at a spot located on the right hand of the central Christ figure.

Knowing that the vanishing point had been deliberately concealed, I focused most of my attention on this general area. What I soon discovered was, by drawing a ring, which has for its center the vanishing point, and extending its circumference out to a point where one of the apostles, second from the right, would appear to be gripping it between his fingers (see blue arrow), some interesting observations can be made.

The first thing I noticed was that the edge of this circle just so happens to precisely intersect the ring finger of not only the twin Christ figure on the left, but also that of one other figure as well. This second figure happens to be the only feminine looking person in this entire group. This woman, who is depicted kneeling on the floor, happens to be holding her left hand in a rather peculiar way, as if the artist wanted to intentionally draw our attention to this particular area. If this is in fact a women, one can only assume, it must be a depiction of Mary Magdelene.

Next, after exploring many options and other possible interpretations, it occurred to me that by drawing in lines connecting the points on these two figures hands, where a wedding ring would typically be placed, with the center of this circle, a very interesting angle is created.

The angle produced by this process is approximately 55 degrees (54.99139 to be exact). Further analysis of this angle reveals it has some very interesting properties and may actually be part of an ancient secret formula used for squaring the circle. The square is constructed by repeating the 55 degree angle every 90 degrees around the circle, then by simply connecting the points where the vector intersects with the circle perimeter (see green dots), and extending those lines to a point where they meet up, at right angles, with the lines that form the adjacent side, a perfect square is created.

The interesting thing about this newly formed square is that the area contained within, calculates out to almost exactly the same area encompassed by the circle. It's important to note, this method for squaring the circle will work regardless of the starting size of the circle and can be accomplished with nothing more than a compass and straightedge. It can also be done in reverse, that is, circling the square or creating a circle whose area equals that of the square. Although it is "mathematically impossible" to exactly match the area of these two geometric shapes, due to the transcendental nature of pi (curves cannot be made straight by numbers), this method does afford its user a quick and easy way to physically, come very very close. This method would definitely provide results good enough for any practical applications such as those used for creating sacred architecture or landscape designs and would be an unvaluable tool for any Master Mason.

Here's an interesting formula regarding the relationship of this angle to the circle:

90 deg(1 qtr circle) - 54.99139 deg = 35.00861 deg

54.99139/35.00861 x 2 = 3.141592 or Pi

One final observation, I find rather interesting, with regards to this construction, is the fact that it produces a likeness of a Templar Cross. This type of cross is the symbol of an organization in which Poussin is rumored to have been a Grand Master. Whether or not this resemblance is by design or just a fluke of the geometry, is for others to decide. All told, it sure looks to be a legitimate possibility.

The Shepherds of Arcadia and The Golden Ratio
By Jim Beck

Much have been written and many theories proposed, in regards to there being some sort of hidden secret geometric armature which Nicolas Poussin used in the creation of one of his greatest works, The Shepherds of Arcadia. Much of this has centred on the positioning and angles of the three staves being held by the shepherds. Theories range from pentagrams, hexagrams and extended pentagrams along with a host of other star-type geometric shapes, not to mention those based on astrological and/or geographical alignments. But to date, none of these have been able to completely and satisfactorily account for all of the features contained in this painting. With that said, here is my attempt at decoding this extraordinary work of art.

This first image shows the basic geometric structure Poussin used in creating his scene. Notice that the center of my outer square is determined by drawing a 45 degree line from the tip of the staff on the far left, down to a point that not only passes perfectly over the top of the middle staff, but just so happens to precisely intersect a bow, formed by the tie straps on the Shepherdess's sandal. This curiosity with the bow prompted me to try doing the same using another bow, this one painted on the sandal of the kneeling shepherd's right foot. Drawing a line from this point at 45 degrees in the opposite direction yielded some very interesting facts. For one, these two perpendicular lines intersected exactly at a line, painted by Poussin, which makes up part of the tomb structure. Also, this point appears to be at the exact horizontal center of the painting. By drawing a line straight up from this intersection, it appears as if the kneeling shepherd is actually pointing to this imaginary line.

Next, using this intersection as my center point, I drew a square, which extends to the very top of the staff depicted on the left. Then, using this same center point, I drew a circle inside this newly formed square. I quickly noticed how the arc of this circle precisely intersected with the top of the staff on the right. Pleased with these results, I continued this pattern by drawing another square that fit exactly in this circle followed by another circle and then another square. At this point, I noticed this last circle and square combination precisely intersected at the center of the bow of the sandal of the kneeling shepherd, and decided this was probably not a random coincidence.

Seeing this, I immediately drew another square from the same center point, only this time causing the corner to intersect at the center of the sandal bow of the shepherdess. Amazingly, this square just so happened to also intersect at the opposite corner with the very top point of the middle staff. It was at this time, I concluded, random coincidence was no longer an option and this construction was undoubtedly by design.

Now it became apparent that Poussin had intended for this last square I had constructed to represent the squaring of the circle. Calculations of the area of these two shapes (both colored black) indicate a very close match, so I have little doubt for this not being Poussin's intention.

Knowing Poussin's passion for incorporating sacred geometry in the structure of his work, I decided to check to see if the Golden Ratio was also a part of this overall plan. What I found was simply incredible. Not only was the Golden Ratio extensively used, it was used in such a way as to define the angle of the right shepherd's staff.

After showing this construction to a friend of mine, I was reminded that various other researchers have made mention of the fact the bottom of the arm of the shepherd on the right, appears to divide the staff he is holding into two equal lengths. This seemed to be intentional on the part of the artist, so I took some measurements. What I discovered was not only did this point represent the exact middle of the staff, but it also defined a vertical Phi ratio of the outer square.

From this basic structure it is easy to see where the angles for the other two staves were derived. Poussin simply used features such as corners or intersections, formed by this construction, as a guide to their positioning.

In conclusion, there may still lie, waiting to be discovered, more secrets hidden within this great work of art. In revealing this construction, it becomes quite evident that Poussin has intentionally concealed his geometric design. His reasons for doing so, one can only assume, were because he had a story to tell, a story which he may not have been welcome to communicate freely in his day. Exactly what this story entails is still not one hundred percent clear. Hopefully, his then unspeakable words, will for not much longer, go unheard.

Chapter 5

Tracking Sirius
By Nicholas R. Mann

Extracts from a new book, 'The Star Temple of Avalon' by Nicholas R. Mann and Philippa Glasson. The Temple Publications, 2007.

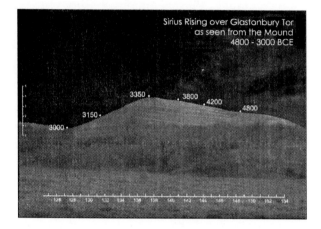

Sirius Rising over Glastonbury Tor as seen from the Mound 4800 - 3000 BCE

The artist Alan Royce shows a figure c 3000 BCE watching Orion rising over Glastonbury Tor from the summit of St Edmund's Hill.

The belt of Orion the Hunter points to the *alpha* star of the constellation Canis Major: this is Sirius, the brightest star in the sky, named in different cultures the Dog, the Heavenly Wolf, the Arrow or Chieftain's Star. Sirius's most visible stellar companion is Orion. These distinctive stars accompany each other around the heavens and the times of their sunrise and sunset risings and settings have been highly significant in all ancient astronomical traditions.

Neolithic Astronomy in Egypt

Egyptian astronomers waited patiently each year for the heliacal rising of Orion, identified with their god Osiris, the 'bringer of life;' then, still more expectantly, for the rising of blue-white Sirius a few days later. For hundreds of years, the first appearance of this brightest and beautiful star, known as *Sepdet* or *Sothis*, signalled the beginning of the inundation of the Nile and the start of the Egyptian New Year. The early cult of this star was linked with the sustenance of the Pharaoh, and hence of the fruitfulness of the land, but it was also seen as offering guidance and protection on the dead ruler's journey to the afterlife. Indeed, Sirius gradually became identified with Osiris' consort, the mother-goddess Isis, or Sothis, who enabled his resurrection.

While initially depicted as a seated cow with a plant between her horns, Sirius is often associated with a jackal or wolf in Graeco-Egyptian culture. Through its connection with the dog, jackal or wolf, Sirius' close affinities with the mysteries of death, judgement and the after-life were strengthened. Egyptologists are still unclear as to whether key temples were oriented to the heliacal rising of Sirius, but strong cases have recently been made for alignments at the archaic temple of Satis at Elephantine, at the temple to Isis in the Dendera complex, and at the 'nest of Horus,' sited at Djebel Thoth above Thebes.[1]

Alone among the fixed stars, Sirius has a 'proper motion' or rate of movement that can provide those who observe it carefully with an almost perfect marker of the true solar year, of 365 and a quarter days. In this respect it acts like a "sun behind the Sun."[2] Each year, in Egypt, when Sirius returned after a seventy day sojourn in the Underworld, it was greeted with celebration as it marked the inauguration of the New Year, and began the procession of the deities who presided over the thirty-six stellar decans. In an esoteric sense, therefore, Sirius opened the pathways of cosmic time, and was truly a leader of the star gods.

Through the Egyptians' careful attention to the greater cycle of Sirius, over a long period of time, it was noticed that it did not continue to rise in the same place. The star was moving slowly across the horizon. In some cases, such as the Temple of Satis at Elephantine and the Temple of Tehuti, or Thoth, at Heliopolis, it seems whole temples may have been dismantled and realigned to the new orientation. Only in recent years, however, has the evidence begun to emerge that this precessional cycle of Sirius was also being watched by our Neolithic British ancestors.

Neolithic Astronomy in Britain

As Neolithic peoples became increasingly familiar with the Isle of Avalon, using its hills to track major solar and lunar cycles, as well as the nightly passage of the 'fixed' stars, they would surely have noticed the gradual movement of Sirius and other key stars along the Eastern horizon over the course of many years. The rate of stellar precession is very slow — it takes seventy-two years for a star to process one degree from its rising place. Yet it was inevitable that the first sky-watchers over Avalon would have noticed the slow precession of Orion and Sirius, especially in their midwinter rising over the Tor after sunset.

In the period 5000 BCE to 3000 BCE, star-watchers upon St Edmund's Hill would have seen the acronychal rising position of Sirius move slowly along the back of the Tor, from South-East to

East. This point eventually coincided with the declination of Winter Solstice sunrise in about 3150 BCE.

In the accompanying figure, we see that in the years around 5000 BCE, when viewed from the summit of what is now St Edmund's Hill, at the Winter Solstice, Sirius was rising at sunset at the lower end of the ridge that forms the southern back of what is now Glastonbury Tor. As people assembled on the hill to greet the shortest day and watch the Winter Solstice sunrise roll up the steep northern side of the Tor, they could have stayed all day and watched the Sun pass over Chalice Hill and set toward Wearyall Hill. Finally, they would have seen Orion rise over the Tor in the gathering twilight. The stars of Orion, notably its 'belt' of three stars, would have indicated the point on the horizon where Sirius would appear a short while later in the gathering night.

A few hundred years later, did an astute sky-watcher notice that Orion's belt was no longer pointing to the same place where they had been taught to expect Sirius to appear? For Sirius, the brightest star in the sky, was now rising marginally higher up the Tor. Of course this was only by an infinitesimal amount, but the back of the Tor would have been perfectly sighted, with no extinction angle, to watch the slow movement of stellar precession.

By 4000 BCE the rising point of Sirius on the Tor was approaching the location of the notch marking the Southern Major Standstill—the lowest rising point of the Moon. By 3500 BCE it was approaching the summit of the Tor. By 3200, the evening rising of Sirius was fast approaching the azimuth of the Winter Solstice rising Sun and finally, by the middle of the century, they were the same.

The Mounds and Monuments

We believe that this coincidence of Sirius and their most significant annual marker, the Winter Solstice Sunrise, would have been seen as signifying a tremendous conjunction of different forces—in an intensification of the mysteries of death and rebirth that Neolithic peoples clearly sought to commemorate in their various monuments.

Firstly, not only do we hold the view that the Mound on St Edmund's Hill in Avalon was built to mark this event in 3150 BCE, but that, secondly, in Egypt, an early temple to the goddess of the Nile flood, Satis, who was closely associated with Sirius, was founded at this time and may have been oriented to this parallel event.[3] Thirdly, in Ireland, the great megalithic chambered mound of Newgrange was built around the same date, between 3300 and 3100 BCE, when not only the light of the Winter Solstice sun but also that of Sirius could illuminate its inner passage on the shortest day.[4] Finally, in Britain, new archaeo-astronomical evidence shows that the second phase of the three great Thornborough Henges in North Yorkshire, dating from c. 3300-3000 BCE, focused attention on the momentous coincidence of the rising of Sirius in the same place as midwinter sunrise.[5]

Wooden posts may have been placed on the back of the Tor in prehistory to help observe the lunar extremes, as well as minute changes in the position of rising stars. The rise in elevation between the Mound and the Tor overcomes the problem of the extinction angle, where stars cannot be seen in the sky due to the atmosphere.

The Heliacal Rising and Setting of Sirius

In 3150 BCE, and as shown in the accompanying figure, we note that for the sky-watchers on the Mound, the heliacal rising of Sirius would have taken place on and around August 23 (in our calendar terms), on the steep northern flank of the Tor. It could have been visible slightly earlier in the month if the skies were clear. The heliacal rising of Sirius is the date in the year when the star first reappears on the eastern horizon, at dawn, just before being extinguished by the growing light of the Sun. For Egyptian astronomers, watching the skies at a more southerly latitude, this reappearance of Sirius took place on and around July 11 in this prehistoric era. As we have mentioned, the event provided them both with a seasonal marker and with a remarkably accurate measurement of the year.

Sirius, like all the 'fixed stars,' is slowly precessing, that is moving slowly around the heavens. As we described above, in 3150 BCE, for a period of about fifty years, the azimuth of the rising of Sirius and that of Winter Solstice sunrise were the same. At that time, Sirius first marked the alignment where the Winter Solstice Sun would rise at dawn in late August, then it gradually rose earlier and earlier, appearing higher and higher in the night sky over the Tor; until, at the Winter Solstice itself, the star was rising after the Sun had set on the south western horizon— accompanying Orion in its full midwinter passage through the sky.

For the astronomers on the 51 degree latitude of the Isle of Avalon, the heliacal setting of Sirius—the setting, not the rising, as shown in the lower half of the picture—would have taken place on or around April 21 in 3150 BCE. The star would have set over Wearyall Hill—on the alignment of the Winter Solstice setting Sun. A star's heliacal setting is the date that it last appears just above the horizon after sunset. The star becomes visible briefly as the Sun's light diminishes before itself setting below the horizon.[6]

With an extinction angle of less than one degree (44 seconds), the brilliant light of Sirius would have been visible to the observers on the Mound low in the sky over Wearyall Hill, until vanishing entirely from view before Sunset on or around what was April 21 in their era. Like the coincidence of its heliacal rising and the Winter Solstice sunrise, and for a period of about fifty years, the azimuth of the heliacal setting of Sirius and that of the Winter Solstice sunset were the same. Observers would have seen Sirius set on the alignment of the Winter Solstice Sun until about April 21, in terms of our calendar; then it was no longer visible until reappearing as the heliacal rising star in late August.

We can only guess at the significance the heliacal rising and setting of Sirius may have had for early British astronomers; yet its disappearance below the horizon would have coincided with the planting of the grain on or around April 21; its reappearance 175 days later coincided with the blessing of the Grain Goddess at the gathering in of the main harvests by August 23. The synchronicity of both these stellar events with the long-observed Winter Solstice alignments near the end of the fourth millennium must have given these times an especial power. For now the ruling star of the harvest, possibly seen as an immensely powerful, yet ambivalent, goddess of fertility and the under-world, coincided with the power of the dying and reborn Sun. The sky-watchers of Avalon must have wondered apprehensively if this momentous event was ushering in an era of greater abundance or of dearth.

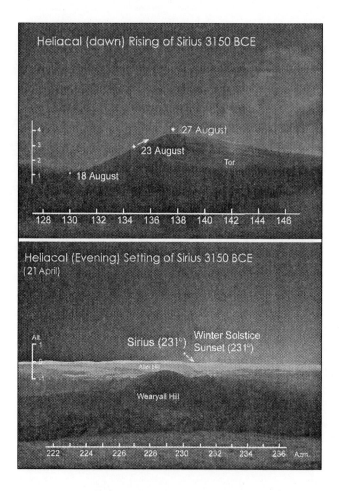

In 3150 BCE the heliacal rising of Sirius began around August 18th;
the star would have been rising strongly by the 23rd. A heliacal
rising is the first appearance of a star on the pre-dawn horizon before
it is extinguished by the light of the Sun. In 3150 BCE the heliacal
rising of Sirius coincided with the alignment of the Winter Solstice
rising Sun. (Today, the heliacal rising of Sirius is closer to an
azimuth of 118° from north.) The lower figure shows the heliacal
setting of Sirius in late April on the Winter Solstice sunset
alignment from the Mound over Wearyall Hill. Sirius would have
been briefly visible for the last time low on the horizon at sunset,

before itself setting below the horizon. This extraordinary coincidence of seasonal markers would have taken place for about fifty years—although the alignments would have appeared roughly coincident for much longer than that, perhaps even a millennium—and led to the building of many complex 'temple' sites.

Gwyn and the Landscape Phenomena
of Glastonbury
By Yuri Leitch

As soon as a book is written it becomes out of date; I learnt this lesson very quickly. When the Temple Publications published my first book back in 2007 (*Gwyn, Ancient god of Glastonbury and Key to the Glastonbury Zodiac*). I thought that I had uncovered pretty much all there was to find upon the given subject - how very wrong I was.

My book revealed an almost forgotten spirit of the Glastonbury mythos. An ancient British god that had been belittled by the centuries into a quaint and twee 'King of the Fairies' - in actuality this genius loci shone forth as a most enigmatic and important British deity. A great Celtic god of old that fellow Gwyn researcher, Dr Angelika Heike Rüdiger, (in issue 12 of *The Temple*) would go on to label as *'Lord of Light & Master of Time'*.

Gwyn's most significant characteristic is that he is the 'Winter King' (the seasonal opposite of the 'Summer King' - who warrants an entire essay of his own and is fruit for future research). To modern pagans the winter king and summer king are celebrated as 'Holly King & Oak King' which, as Dr Rüdiger's work clearly shows, is an ancient tradition throughout northern Europe and further a field - see her deeply detailed article *'Gwyn ap Nudd: A First and Frame Deity'* in issue 13 of *The Temple*.

The Winter King governs the six months of the year from the 1st of November (Samhain) until the 1st of May (Beltaine) and he is symbolically represented in the heavens by the constellation that we now call Orion the Hunter - which in the northern hemisphere governs the winter months and disappears below the horizon throughout the summer months.

As my *Gwyn* book discloses, the very unique landscape in and around Glastonbury has certain magnificent 'Winter king' functions that can still be observed to this very day - the machinery of the ancients still operates!

The Landscape Phenomena of Glastonbury

1 - Orion's hunting
2 - The Beltaine Line
3 - The Winter Solstice Sun Roll
4 - The Glastonbury Zodiac
5 - New Revelations

1 Orion's Hunting - throughout the winter evenings the constellation of Orion (Gwyn) appears to rise out of Glastonbury Tor, into the night sky, fulfilling the legends of Gwyn ap Nudd's wild hunts during winter nights! This phenomenon can be observed from the town centre but also, most importantly, from the location of the native British Iron Age Lake Village - this angle of perspective is also that of the Winter Solstice alignment (see Sun Roll further on and accompanying Map).

2 The Beltaine Line - (more commonly known as the 'St. Michael Line') is probably the most famous 'Ley-line' in Britain; first brought to public awareness by the late John Michell in the 1960's and then triumphed in the best selling book *The Sun & the Serpent* by Paul Broadhurst and Hamish Miller. Stretching across the landscape in a northeasterly direction from St. Michael's Mount in Cornwall, all the way to St Margaret's ruined church of Hopton-on-Sea upon the Norfolk Coast, incorporating many St. Michael churches along its way. The directional alignment of this 'Michael Line' points to sunrise on May the 1st (the Celtic Fire Festival of Beltaine).

I believe it was John Michell that gave this magnificent alignment the nickname of the 'St. Michael Line'. In the *Sun & the*

Serpent the authors dowsed two separate bands of energy which they then described as the 'Michael Line' and the 'Mary Line', this has lead people to call the alignment the 'Michael & Mary Line' - in my opinion this is an error that gives the Line a flavour of Christianity that is very misleading as many powerful sacred sites of ancient pagan origin (like the Hurlers stone circle in Bodmin, the Avebury complex and Glastonbury Tor itself) create this magnificent alignment that points to sunrise on the 1st of May. The churches are but flags of ownership placed by a later (Norman) tradition.

Churches of course, are often built upon the earlier sites of pagan sanctity, especially upon prominent hilltops as with the 'St. Michael' churches of the 'Michael Line'. The Line has also been called 'The Great Dragon Line' but how this nickname came about I am uncertain. Understanding the Beltaine traditions of Glastonbury Tor (that is itself located roughly midway along the Line) I share the growing belief that the Line should simply be called the 'Beltaine Line'.

Until the discovery of the 'Beltaine Line' the May Day significance of Glastonbury Tor was not generally known about in public consciousness until the 1960's but it was known about to the few. In issue 10 of *The Temple*, in an article called *'The Somerset Parallelogram'*, I explained the probable revelation of the 'Beltaine Line' given in the writings of the esoteric occultist Katharine Emma Maltwood in the 1930's. Katharine was the first person to write about the hidden significance of St. Michael churches upon hilltops and about the Beltaine fire beacons upon Glastonbury Tor.

"... It must have been an inspiring sight when Glastonbury Tor stood in the midst of hundreds of Beacon Fires tossing their flames up to the night sky from the surrounding hills, a survival of the Beltane Fires of May Day."
('Temple of the Stars' by Katharine Maltwood)

The pagan sanctity of Glastonbury Tor (and Chalice Well) is a vision shared by Katharine's more famous contemporary occultist Dion Fortune,

"There can be little doubt that the priests of the ancient sun-worship had here their holy place. The Tor is a strange hill, and it is hard to believe that its form is wholly the work of Nature. Round it winds a spiral way in three great coils, which was beyond all question a processional way. When did the Christians worship upon high places? Never. But such mounts as this were always sacred to the sun. It is the natural place for a sun-temple, and for the great fires of the kindred fire-worship."
('Avalon of the Heart' by Dion Fortune)

Both Katharine Maltwood and Dion Fortune were living around Glastonbury in the 1920's and 30's. Both speak of the significance of fire beacons upon the Tor and Katharine specifically mentions Beltaine, St. Michael churches and I am sure that her landscape geometry revelations lead to the discovery of the Beltaine Alignment.

Because the Beltaine Line is a physical thing, a thing that can be looked at, measured, touched and walked upon, it is fair to describe it as having an objective physical reality. Thus, of all the legends that surround Glastonbury the Beltaine alignment is the primary key to unlocking the door to Glastonbury's inner sanctum. It was this understanding that fired my imagination, allowing me to bypass the Grail glamour of the Joseph of Arimathea legend and the medieval contrivance of King Arthur's Grave - both stories being Abbey invented legends that shed no light what-so-ever upon the Beltaine alignment. Only the obscure Welsh traditions of Gwyn ap Nudd, King of the Fairies, upon Glastonbury Tor - who has a perpetual battle, every May Day (Beltaine) until the day of doom hinted at shedding any light upon the mystery of the Beltaine Line. How could it be that medieval Welsh stories remembered the Beltaine traditions of Glastonbury? This question lead me to writing my Gwyn book, in truth, once the question was asked, the book wrote itself. In short, Glastonbury Tor is the abode of Gwyn ap Nudd, the British 'Winter King' who has an annual battle every Beltaine and this hill of the Winter King is itself situated upon the most important Beltaine aligned ley-line in the country!

3 The Winter Solstice Sun Roll - is the third Winter King piece of sacred landscape phenomena at Glastonbury. It is a truly magnificent and wonderful creation of landscape engineering. Once viewed by the naked eye it pierces the heart and stays with you forever. Sadly, because it happens during midwinter in Britain, more times than not the magic is obscured by mist, fog, rain or cloud. In 2006 I was one of the lucky few (less than twenty) to stand upon the viewing mound on top of Edmund's Hill, on a cold but clear blue winter morning and I watched the sun take thirty minutes to slowly, beautifully and perfectly roll up the eastern slope of Glastonbury Tor to its summit - just mind-blowing. It was not visible due to bad weather in 2007 or 2008 but more and more people are turning up, full of hope. In 2008 at least fifty hopefuls gathered on a cloudy day, the next time it is clear weather there will be hundreds of people there.

In short, every Winter Solstice (21st December) when the sun is reborn and the days start to grow in length again, the new sun rolls up the Winter King's hill! Nicholas R Mann & Philippa Glasson writes about this great enigma in great depth in their book *'The Star Temple of Avalon'*.

4 The Glastonbury Zodiac - gives us yet another piece of Winter King enigma. On its own a very subjective and improvable thing but when added to Orion's Rising, the Beltaine Line and the Winter Solstice Sun Roll, the Gwyn ap Nudd connections to the Glastonbury Zodiac are unnerving and sit in the brain like an itch that cannot be ignored.

It was Katharine Maltwood (the revealer of the Beltaine Line) that discovered the Glastonbury Zodiac during the 1920's - or so she claimed. This Somerset Zodiac itself is a complicated mystery of many intricacies - the story of which is currently being put together by my friend Oddvar Olsen and myself. We aim to have 'The High History of the Somerset Star Temple' published in the spring of 2010.

In short, Katharine Maltwood claimed to of discovered a vast Star Temple of landscape effigies that represented the zodiacal (and other) constellations upon the ground - a huge circular design over ten miles wide! Katharine's theory came up against much ridicule and is still dismissed by academia today but more esoterically minded people believe that it has a certain reality - for myself, some days I believe in it, other days I don't but the histories and mysteries that seemingly interconnect with it are irresistible to the curiously minded. It may not exist but it will never go away! Which in itself may be Katharine's biggest act of genius. An esoteric sculptress who was well versed in eastern mysticism and well skilled at creating intricate designs, or was she an honest pilgrim investigating the land?

Whatever the case may be, obscure Welsh Triads, compiled more than a hundred years before Katharine Maltwood discovered the Glastonbury Zodiac, describe Gwyn ap Nudd as being on of the top three Astronomers of the Isle of Britain!

"The three renowned astronomers of the Isle of Britain: Idris the giant; Gwydion son of Don; and Gwyn son of Nudd. Such was their knowledge of the stars, their natures and qualities, that they could prognosticate whatever was wished to be known until the day of doom."

(From the compilation of Iolo Morganwg, published in 1807)

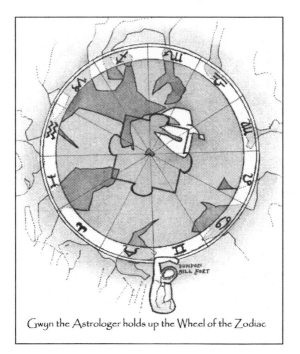

Gwyn the Astrologer holds up the Wheel of the Zodiac

Until the day of doom' is a fascinating statement that also occurs in the Mabinogion story of Gwyn's annual Beltaine battle, which must happen perpetually until the day of doom. It is this clue and other 'time' aspects that have lead Dr Rüdiger to describe Gwyn as the 'Master of Time'.

In Katharine's landscape Star Temple she places the constellation of Orion (Gwyn) as a giant lying among the Somerset Levels. His big belly is Lollover Hill and his head is the Iron Age hill-fort of Dundon Beacon - the closest hill-fort to Glastonbury Tor. The Orion (Gwyn) effigy holds aloft in his upturned hand the great ring of the zodiacal constellations (see illustration) he is the Time Lord holding secure the Gateway of the Stars!

5 New Revelations

Always there will be new discoveries. Some turn your established opinions up side down others lend weight, in unexpected ways, to your established train of thought - and so the adventures unfold. I must thank Dr Angelika Rüdiger for pointing me in the direction of a little known archaeological survey, the potential ramifications of which are massively important to the understanding of Glastonbury Tor as the centre of a sacred landscape.

The Pagan Temple on Top of Glastonbury Tor - In 2001, local Consultant Archaeologists, Charles & Nancy Hollinrake, presented an *'An Archaeological and Historical Survey of St. Michael's Church Tower, Glastonbury Tor, including a re-interpretation of the summit excavation and a Fabric Survey of the Structure by J. Sampson.'* to The National Trust. In this survey the National Trust were given the very strong evidence for the existence of a circular Romano British pagan temple on the top of Glastonbury Tor. To this very day (summer 2009) eight years in passing, the National Trust have sat on this survey and done nothing with it. The tourist information boards at the foot of the Tor (which are new) do not even say that there was 'possibly' a Pagan Temple on the Tor - this important information remains silent and until now unpublished (I understand that the Hollinrake's are currently in the process of writing their own book about the subject.)

It would be perfectly in keeping with the local area, in the Romano British period, for the Tor to have a temple sited upon it. There are many sites of Roman temples (on hill tops) in the area - Brean Down, Pagan's Hill and Lamyatt, to name just a few. Gwyn's own father, Nudd, has a Temple site a Lydney on the River Severn. In fact, it would be odd, and beyond expectation, for the Tor not to have a Roman temple upon it. What with its very close proximity to the Fosse Way, it being the most dominant single hill for miles around and blessed with many natural springs of fresh water - not to mention Roman finds in every single archaeological dig, dug, in and around Glastonbury.

In paragraph 6.7 of the survey it reads,

'The postulated Romano-Celtic temple or shrine would also explain another class of artefact recorded during the excavations, that is hundreds of ammonite fossils found on the summit...'

In a phone conversation I had with Nancy Hollinrake I asked her how many hundreds of ammonites were found on the summit of the Tor and she told me *'at least four hundred!'* Ammonites are found in the area but to find four hundred or so, seemingly, deliberately, piled together, is a very odd thing to say the least. The theory is that they are the remains of many votive offerings.

Here is the very peculiar thing. As has been already established, the Winter King attributes of the Tor have been discussed along with the astronomical connections with Gwyn ap Nudd. The Winter Solstice sun rolling up the hill is an absolutely objective truth. Now then; Winter Solstice, every year (until the day of doom) is defined by the moment when the sun appears to enter into the sign of Capricorn - in classical tradition often equated with the horny god Pan.

Capricorn means 'Goat's Horn'. Ammonites, since classical times, have represented ram's horns! The word ammonite itself is derived from 'Horns of Ammon' (a ram-horned god of ancient Egypt. So we now have over four hundred ram's horn votive offerings on the Winter King's hill that correspond directly to Winter Solstice and the sun entering Capricorn! If this weren't strange enough, that in the landscape at the eastern foot of the Tor (from where rises the mid winter sun) lays Katharine Maltwood's landscape effigy of Capricorn!

The White Hart - The landscape where lays Katharine Maltwood's effigy of Capricorn is today called Hearty Moor. It used to be wetland area and is now irrigated for farming. The Whitelake River still runs through these fields and becomes the Hartlake area of the Levels on the north side of the Isle of Glastonbury - before joining up with the River Brue near the site of the Iron Age Lake Village.

Along with place names like Harter's Hill and Hearty Moor, the names Whitelake and Hartlake seem to suggest 'White Hart' an idea promoted by the late Mary Caine in her book *'The Glastonbury Zodiac'*. Because of this I had begun to ponder the idea that the White Hart could be a symbol for Gwyn ap Nudd (the name Gwyn is simply Welsh for 'White').

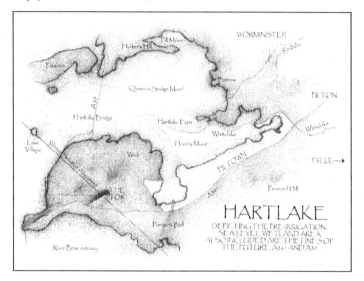

It would seem that a Winter King should be horned because of Capricorn (and the four hundred ammonites being a possible *interpretatio Romano* of the native British view of the Tor). Looking around what little horned god imagery there is for Celtic Europe, Stag's antlers seem to be the natural 'horns' for this part of the world. So seeing Gwyn as the 'antlered white one' it seems to me all too obvious that the White Hart should be his symbol.

In Druidic tradition the appearance of the White Hart means that the Otherworld is very close by. It is also said that the White Hart acts as a messenger and guide between this world and the Otherworld - characteristics shared with Gwyn ap Nudd who is often described as Lord of the Otherworld and King of the Fairies. According to Arthurian author John Whitehead, in his book *'Guardian of the Grail'*,

> *"... the White Hart is the name and symbol of the old British religion, or preferably social philosophy, for it contained nothing mystic but simply common-sense principles for a happy life... it is the change from that old philosophy to the new faith, from the creed of the White Hart to that of the Cross which constitutes the tale of knightly adventures in the romantic legend of the Grail..."*

In the Mabinogion story of *'Peredur'* the mysterious and fae Empress (Goddess of the land) reprimands Peredur for beheading her magical stag, telling him that he had killed *'the most beautiful jewel in her land'*; in penance for which she sends Peredur off on a quest which leads him to achieving his own journey's end.

Herne the Hunter - in the 14th century King Richard II took the White Hart to be his royal emblem, most likely because of the story of Herne the Hunter.

Herne was a royal huntsman loyal to the king. One day whilst hunting the king was suddenly attacked by a fierce White Hart. Herne threw himself between the king and the Hart and saved the kings life - in so doing Herne was mortally wounded and lay upon the ground dying. A wizard appeared, the Hart was slain, and the wizard healed Herne by attaching the Hart's antlers onto Herne's head - where they stayed for the rest of his life. Herne lived for many years and was the chief huntsman of Windsor Castle. Legend says that one day he was framed for a crime that he did not commit - for which he was hung to death upon a mighty oak tree in Windsor Park. It is said that his ghost still haunts the land and even William Shakespeare wrote about him in his *'Merry Wives of Windsor'*,

'Sometime a keeper here in Windsor Forest,
Doth all the winter-time at still midnight,
Walk round about an oak, with great ragg'd horns;
And there he blasts the tree, and takes the cattle,
And makes milch-kine yield blood, and shakes a chain,
In a most hideous and dreadful manner.
You have heard of such a spirit, and well you know
The superstitious idle-headed eld
Receiv'd and did deliver to our age,
This tale of Hearne the Hunter for truth.

Herne the Hunter shares many characteristics with Gwyn ap Nudd. They are both wintertime hunters, they both ride a black horse and they are both said to be accompanied by an owl.

The old medieval market cross of Glastonbury used to be topped by a curious effigy of a man (believed to of been representative of Bacchus, the Roman god of wine) but nick-named by locals as 'Jack Stagg' - now kept in the Abbey museum.

For many centuries the most important inn in Glastonbury (and earlier entrance to the Abbey grounds) was the 'White Hart' - it is now the Assembly Rooms.

Herne the Hunter's spirit found a great revival as 'Lord of the Trees' in the hit, 1980's, TV series *'Robin of Sherwood'* - the haunting image of the stag-headed man resonated deeply with pagan-hearted Britons of the twentieth century, and indeed, still does to this day.

Herne still acts as a protector of the land. It is said that his ghost will appear as a warning at times of national crisis. The antler-headed god is an ancient Celtic image of pre-Roman Europe. As John Whitehead observes (in his above mentioned book) Herne the Hunter was,

"... the anglicised designation of the Cerne druid of the stag-headed deity Cernunnos."

Cernunnos is a Romanised, continental Celtic, name; most probably derived from Herne or Cerne - there are many Herne and Cerne place names in Britain (even beside Glastonbury's 'Hartlake' lies 'Hearne House' and 'Hearne Farm'). Janet & Stewart Farrar, in their book *'The Complete Dictionary of European Gods & Goddesses'*, say,

"It has been suggested that the name Herne was adopted from the mating call of a doe for her buck—approximately 'Hurrrn!' - on the natural assumption that if that was what she called him, that was his name."

Chapter 5 Tracking Sirius References:

1   Shaltout M., & Belmonte, J.A., JHA, PP 03 (2005), On the Orientations of Ancient Egyptian Temples I: Upper Egypt and Lower Nubia, passim.

2   Bomhard, Anne-Sophie von, (1999), The Egyptian Calendar: A Work for Eternity, London: Periplus, pp. 32-45.

3   Shaltout and Belmonte (2005), p. 7.

4   The length of time Sirius would have visible from within Newgrange would have been determined by the size of the aperture or 'light box' over the entrance.

5   Harding, Jan, (2003), Henge Monuments of the British Isles, Stroud: Tempus Books. Also, forthcoming book on Thornborough in 2007.

6   The helical rising or setting of a star was identified with the point in the year when the star would be briefly visible just before sunrise or just after sunset. The last time this took place at sunset is called the acronychal rising and the first time at dawn, the cosmical setting. Note: It is generally the case that there needs to be at least eleven degrees between the star and the Sun (below the horizon) for the star not to be drowned in the solar glare. With the extinction angle, only the very brightest of stars can appear near markers on a low horizon in a bright sky.

About the Authors

Stephen Andrews is a local government officer and environmentalist with twenty-five years service in 'Town and Country Planning and Conservation'. He lives in Suffolk with his wife, two sons and three old motorbikes. Over thirty years he has travelled the pilgrim's routes of Europe. Stephen is an avid researcher, and author of several articles.

Sylvia P. Beamon, M.A. (Cantab) studied archaeology and anthropology, graduating from Cambridge University in 1977(Lucy Cavendish College). She has held a long-term interest in underground structures and the reuse of the galleries and chambers left within disused mines. She has lectured and published widely in this field. Sylvia founded the national society Subterranea Britannica in 1974 editing its journal of the same name for ten years.

Sylvia co-authored *The Ice-houses of Britain* (1990) Routledge, London which is recognised as the definitive work on Icehouses in this country. The National Monuments Record and the British Academy supported the project, with Dr Susan Roaf, which gained a British Archaeological Award in 1986.

In addition to her roles as book reviewer, archaeological excavator, TV / radio contributor and conference organiser, Sylvia has interests in childcare and health issues. Since 1996, she has become a reviewer and consumer for the Cochrane Collaboration and continues research into the underground treatment of asthma known as Speleotherapy.

Other titles by Sylvia include: *Royston Cave Used by Saint or Sinners? The Ice-houses of Britain, Exploring Royston Cave, Underground Mythology* and *Speleotherapy for Asthma*

Jim Beck is author of numerous articles and has for many years studied the Knights Templar and the mysteries surrounding Rennes-Le-Chateau. His speciality is sacred geometry.

Paul Broadhurst is one of Britain's leading mythologists and researchers into ancient landscapes. Among his books are the seminal *The Sun and The Serpent*, which has become a classic in its field, and its sequel, *The Dance of the Dragon*. *The Green Man and the Dragon* explores the myth behind the mystery of St George and other dragon-slaying legends. Soon to be published is *The Secret Land - The Origins of Arthurian Legend and the Grail Quest*, the product of ten years of research in the landscape of the British Westcountry, which includes some of the most remarkable discoveries ever uncovered. www.mythospress.co.uk

Terence F. Dick is a writer and reseacher, now a retired engineer based in Worthing, Sussex. Was a member of the CBA - Council for British Archaeology. A researcher in unusual drawing designs combining engineering drawing skills in specific research areas of archaeology and history. Took part in an indepth study of the renowned Sumerian gaming boards and pieces of ancient UR at the British Museum based on Sumerian culture.

Juliet Faith has had an interest in the Knights Templar for many years. She has spent the last three years writing a book about the Templar's in Somerset, her home county. Her book entitled *'The Knights Templar in Somerset'*, is to be published later this year.

Atasha Fyfe is a past life regressionist and writer living in Glastonbury. She can be contacted by e-mail at: atafymail-pastlives@yahoo.co.uk

Philip Gardiner is published in several languages including English, Czech, Romanian, Greek, Polish, Portuguese, Spanish, Italian, German, Estonian and many more. His books include: *The Serpent Grail, The Shining Ones, Gnosis: The Secret of Solomon's Temple Revealed, The Ark, The Shroud and Mary, Secret Societies, Gateways to the Otherworld, The Bond Code, Secrets of the Serpent, What Wise Men Do* and a fiction entitled *Brotherhood of the Snake.* He has made several award winning documentaries, appeared on both Discovery and History Channel. He also hosts his own TV Chat Show in the UK called Gardiner's World. His website is www.gardinersworld.com. He has a BA in Marketing and is Vice President of Reality Films. He writes a regular column for a prestigious London arts magazine, as well as regular contributions to dozens of magazines worldwide.

Callum Jensen is an author and researcher who has written two books under the pseudonym Dan Green, 'The Lincoln Da Vinci Code' (2005) and 'The Lincoln Da Vinci Code and the mystery of Rennes-le-Chateau' (2006). He has been rearching the Rennes mystery since 1986. His related Youtube short films can be found at: www.youtube.com/greenren07

Forrest D. Lamb is a teacher, a therapist and a lifelong Arthurian enthusiast. He graduated from Canterbury Christ Church University with First Class Honours in Religious Studies. A trained teacher and hypnotherapist, Forrest now lives happily stateside with his wife, teens and Patterdale Terrier in beautiful Portland, Oregon. Though, he often longs for the misty moors of Somerset and the four wonderful years he lived in the shadow of the Tor.

Yuri Leitch is the author of the best selling *GWYN - Ancient god of Glastonbury and key to the Glastonbury Zodiac* and co author of *The High History of the Somerset Temple*. For many years Yuri has written essays and articles, for various publications on a range of topics. His knowledge grows as he researches and encompasses the stories of the ancient deities, his own Holy Grail investigations and related esoteric matters.

Yuri lives in Glastonbury, Somerset, where he works as an author and artist. He also spends many of his hours with his head stuck in dusty old books and has made a passionate study of British History, Celtic Folklore and a broad spectrum of the world's ancient mythologies for over twenty years. He was born in Barnstaple, Devon, in 1968, and has spent most of his life living in the South West of Britain. He has explored the landscape and histories of the Isles of Scilly, Cornwall, the Cotswolds, Bristol and Avon and now Somerset. If visiting Glastonbury pop in to view his art-work in his studio *Spiritvisions* in Monarch's Way.

Evelyn Lord. Before her retirement, she was course director of the masters in local and regional history, University of Cambridge. She has published widely on local history and is the author of *The Knights Templar in Britain* and *The Stuart Secret Army*. At present she is an emeritus fellow of Wolfson College, and is working on a book on 20th century Suffolk.

Nicholas R. Mann is an internationally published author of many books including *The Isle of Avalon, The Star Temple of Avalon, The Sacred Geometry of Washington DC, The Keltic Power Symbols* and *Sedona: Sacred Earth*. He lives in Glastonbury.

Hugh Montgomery was educated both in the UK and abroad, after a successful business career in South America, Africa and the Middle East, as well as the UK, Hugh Montgomery returned to Academia becoming President of and Professor at the Megatrend University of Applied Sciences in Belgrade, formerly Yugoslavia now Serbia. He retired from the position of President some five years ago, but remains on the board of overseas Professors. In 2005 he was elected a Fellow of the prestigious Society of Antiquaries of Scotland, Scotland's oldest learned Society, founded in 1780. In retirement he continues to work for the local community being recently elected a local councillor.

Professor Montgomery holds a Ph.D. in Audiology, a Diploma in Contract Law and the professional qualification of Inginiero Comercial (Chile). He is the author of a number of technical and historical papers and books including *The Montgomery Millennium, The God-Kings of Europe* and *The God Kings of England.*

Oddvar Olsen has studied mythologies, the occult, various mystery traditions and the Knights Templars since the late eighties. He has travelled extensively throughout Asia, Africa and Europe before he settled in Somerset in 1999. In 2002 he started the successful *'The Temple'* (www.thetemplebooklet.co.uk); a periodical dedicated to the Knights Templar and related subjects.

Olsen is the editor of *The Templar Papers,* and co-author of *The High History of the Somerset Temple.* In 2007 he set up a publishing company: The Temple Publications Ltd. (www.thetemplepublications.com)

BOOKS

O is a symbol of the world, of oneness and unity. In different cultures it also means the "eye," symbolizing knowledge and insight. We aim to publish books that are accessible, constructive and that challenge accepted opinion, both that of academia and the "moral majority."

Our books are available in all good English language bookstores worldwide. If you don't see the book on the shelves ask the bookstore to order it for you, quoting the ISBN number and title. Alternatively you can order online (all major online retail sites carry our titles) or contact the distributor in the relevant country, listed on the copyright page.

See our website www.o-books.net for a full list of over 500 titles, growing by 100 a year.

And tune in to myspiritradio.com for our book review radio show, hosted by June-Elleni Laine, where you can listen to the authors discussing their books.

mySpiritRadio